Ephesus

Ephesus

The Nursery of Christianity

Edgar Stubbersfield

WIPF & STOCK · Eugene, Oregon

EPHESUS
The Nursery of Christianity

Copyright © 2022 Edgar Stubbersfield. All rights reserved. Except for brief quotations in critical publications or reviews, no part of this book may be reproduced in any manner without prior written permission from the publisher. Write: Permissions, Wipf and Stock Publishers, 199 W. 8th Ave., Suite 3, Eugene, OR 97401.

Wipf & Stock
An Imprint of Wipf and Stock Publishers
199 W. 8th Ave., Suite 3
Eugene, OR 97401

www.wipfandstock.com

PAPERBACK ISBN: 978-1-6667-4132-2
HARDCOVER ISBN: 978-1-6667-4133-9
EBOOK ISBN: 978-1-6667-4134-6

12/13/22

This book is dedicated to Jim McDonald
A Police Officer, Councilor, Mayor, and Member of Parliament
but above all a friend when I needed one.

Contents

Abbreviations | viii

Ephesus, the Nursery of Christianity | 1
1. Geography | 3
2. Ephesian History | 7
3. Ephesian Freedom | 35
4. Ephesian Artemis | 39
5. Other Pagan Religions | 77
6. Judaism and Christianity in Ephesus | 100
7. Conclusion | 111

Source of Illustrations | 112
Bibliography | 115

Abbreviations

1 Apol	First Apology
Anc	Res Gestae Divi Augusti (Monumentum Ancyranum)
Ag. Ap.	Against Apion
Ann.	The Annals
Ant.	Antiquities of the Jews
Anth. Pal.	Palatine Anthology (Greek Anthology)
Cal.	Gaius Caligula
De Arch.	On Architecture
Demetr.	Life of Demetrius
Descr.	Description of Greece
Eph.	To the Ephesians
Geogr.	Geography
Haer.	Against Heresies
HH.	Homeric Hymns
Hist.	The Histories
Hist. eccl.	Ecclesiastical History
Hist. rom.	Roman History
Hymn Del.	Hymn to Delos
Hymn. Dian.	Hymns to Diana or Artemis
Imag.	Imagines
Leuc. Clit.	The Adventures of Leucippe and Clitophon

ABBREVIATIONS

Mil. Glo.	*Miles Gloriosus* (The Braggart Captain)
Mith.	*Mithridatic Wars*
Nat.	*The Natural Histories*
Nat. an.	*On the Nature of Animals*
Or.	*Orations*
Sat.	*Satires*
Var. hist.	*Various Histories*
Vit. Apoll.	*Life of Apollonius of Tyana*
Vit. Soph.	*Life of the Sophists*

Ephesus, the Nursery of Christianity

WELCOME TO THE LONG-ABANDONED glories of the Greek city of Ephesus in what is now Turkey. While Jerusalem has been called the cradle of Christianity, Ephesus was surely its nursery. One writer summed up the importance of this city to Christianity when he said, "for one momentous generation, Ephesus was the literary focus of early Christianity, and by its compilations . . . influenced Christianity more than Jerusalem, Antioch, or Rome."[1] This ancient city played a pivotal part in the formation of the New Testament with at least six of its books having or claiming to have a connection. Paul ministered in Ephesus longer than in any other city and legend has it that John lived the last of his very long life in Ephesus. It is also where these same legends say that Timothy became the city's first bishop and was martyred and where the runaway slave Onesimus[2] would eventually succeed him. Legend also says that Mary, the mother of Jesus, saw out her last days in this city.

The provenance and even the recipients of some of the New Testament letters is contested, but the traditional understanding of the authorship and recipients or destinations of the letters shows a very strong association with Ephesus as:

- Both Corinthian letters were written from here,
- Romans was written shortly after Paul left Ephesus,[3]

---

1. Goodspeed, *New Chapters*, 49.
2. Ign. *Eph.* 6.
3. It is suggested that our letter to the Romans may actually be a copy of

EPHESUS: THE NURSERY OF CHRISTIANITY

- First and Second Timothy were written to Paul's assistant ministering in Ephesus,
- There is a letter bearing the name of the city,
- John's Gospel and letters are associated with his stay in Ephesus, and
- The Apocalypse was written on an island close to Ephesus.

If Paul wrote his prison epistles from Ephesus,[4] Colossians, Philemon, and Philippians would also be associated with the city. Colossae, also in Asia Minor, was about 200 kilometers from Ephesus but was connected by important trade routes and the Lycus River so its culture would have been similar.

I hope you enjoy this short trip back to a world and culture that was very different from our own. Without an understanding of this city, its lifestyles, and the beliefs of its community and of those living in locations around it, we cannot start to comprehend what theologians call the *sitzenbleiben*. We would simply refer to the life situation that Paul and John were writing into. Without understanding what the books said to the intended recipients we can easily read into them a meaning not necessarily intended by the author.

---

the original that was sent to Ephesus as the greetings in the final chapter are to people we expect to be living in Asia. Koester, "Ephesus," 123.

4. Now widely but not universally accepted.

1. Geography

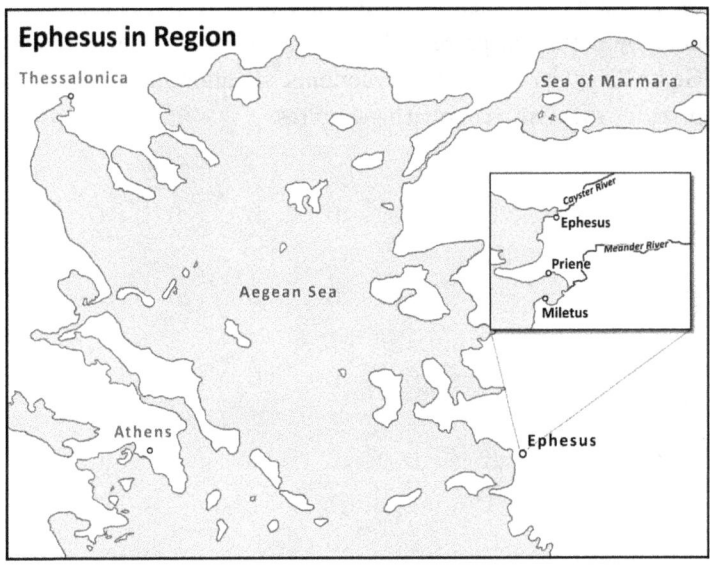

Location of Ephesus

IT IS HARD TO comprehend that the archaeological site of Ephesus, which is now eight kilometers inland, was once one of the ancient world's great seaports! In classical times, Ephesus was essentially a coastal city situated on the Cayster River (also known as the Küçük Menderes) in Anatolia, Turkey, between where it empties into the Aegean Sea and the Koressos Mountains. Long after the founding of Ephesus, Polybius wrote about its strategic importance saying, "King Antiochus was very anxious to get possession of Ephesus because of its favorable site, as it may be said to stand in the position of a citadel both by land and sea for anyone with designs on Ionia and the cities of the Hellespont and is always a most favorable point of defense against Europe for the kings of Asia."[1]

Ephesus, which faced the Greek world to the west, was ideally situated for commerce. Strabo,[2] the great Greek geographer, wrote that Ephesus's location with an accessible harbor and being effectively the start of the Persian royal road was the main reasons for its economic growth and rise to prominence.[3] Further, with the city also being sited on the north-south coastal road, and with links by mountain passes to the Hermos River Valley (Modern Gediz River) its strategic and economic situation made Ephesus a prize for successive conquering empires.

---

1. Polybius, *Histories*, 18.40a. Polybius (ca. 200–118 BC) was a historian of the Hellenistic period and is important because of his discussion of the separation of powers in government.

2. Strabo (ca. 54 BC–AD 24), a native of Pontus studied philosophy and became a Stoic. He was an eyewitness of much of his geographical information making it invaluable for people in the higher departments of administration and international politics. He was well-acquainted with history and the mythological traditions of his nation and was a devout admirer of Homer and acquainted with the other great poets.

3. Strabo, *Geogr.* 14.1.24. The road was likely not paved till Roman times.

1. GEOGRAPHY

Aerial view of Ephesus showing the Roman harbor and canal connecting it to the Cayster River

Three hills, now known as Panayir Dagh (155 meters and central in the aerial view), Bulbul Dagh (358 meters and to the right in the aerial view), and Ayasoluk (near the Temple of Artemis known as the Artemision), govern the topography with the city built on their slopes and between their narrow valleys. This topography and the silting of earlier harbors[4] dictated the growth of the city and its water supply. Refer to pages 26 and 27 for their location.[5]

The city tourists know as Ephesus was not the Ephesus of classical Greece but was moved because the original city was not built in an ideal location. It was first situated near the Artemision, and was built on the floodplain of the Marnas (modern Degirmen) and Selinous (modern Abu-hayat) rivers. These two rivers could flood the whole plain at times. The situation by the fourth century BC has been described as, "when it was not flooded, the

---

4. Zabehlicky, "Preliminary Views," 202.

5. A larger topographical map with details that are easier to read can be found at https://web.archive.org/web/20210628014030/http://homepage.uni-vie.ac.at/elisabeth.trinkl/forum/forum0897/04plan.htm.

area directly south and east of the Artemision must have been wet in winter, swampy during the spring, and generally pestilential during the summer."[6]

---

6. Rogers, *Mysteries of Artemis*, 65.

2. Ephesian History

The Name, Ephesus

Silver tetradrachm ca. 405–325 BC

LITTLE IS KNOWN OF the prehistory of the city though Mycenaean graves and artefacts (1400–1500 BC) have been found indicating a long settlement period. As well, Hittite cuneiform tablets have been found at Miletus[1] which refer to a village *Apasus*, possibly this city.[2] Not surprisingly, the origin of the city's name has been lost in time, but it may derive from *apis*, which is Greek for "bee" and the city did have a strong association with bees in its

---

1. Another Greek port city in Asia Minor and about 46 kilometers south of Ephesus.
2. McDonald, "Ephesus," 318.

iconography and terminology. Some of its coins carried the image of a bee[3] and Ephesian hoplites, heavily armed foot soldiers, are known to have the bee on their shields.[4]

The priestesses and chief priest at the temple of Artemis were known as *melissai*, another Greek word for bee, and the King Bee respectively.[5] Alternatively, Artemis Ephesia was the full name of the leading local deity which could also explain the city's name, i.e., it is named after the god, not the god after the city. The goddess' name is also said to come from a Greek adjective meaning "safe and sound"[6] which would be an ideal name for a city which makes people feel *artimeas*. Pausanias[7] refers to the founding of the first large temple in the city by Croesus[8] and a man called Ephesus "who was thought to be a son of the river Cayster."[9] This is also a suggested origin of the name. Strabo says the name originates from the Amazons though he does not say how.[10]

Mythological Founding of Ephesus

Strabo visited Ephesus not many years before Paul.[11] He records in his *Geography*,[12] both the historical and the mythological accounts of the founding of the city. The myth links Ephesus to Smyrna, an Amazon, a member of the mythological race of fierce women

3. McDonald, "Ephesus," 318.
4. Skarmintzo, "Cult of Artemis," 271.
5. Burrell, "Bee and the Deer," para. 3.
6. Strabo, *Geogr.* 14.1.6.
7. Pausanias was a second-century mythographer and travel writer.
8. Croesus was king of Lydia in what is now Turkey from 560–547 BC. The old expression, "as rich as Croesus" refers to him. He is credited with minting the first gold coins of standard weight and purity.
9. Pausanias, *Descr.* 7.2.7.
10. Strabo says, "Smyrna was an Amazon who took possession of Ephesus; and hence the name both of the inhabitants and of the city, just as certain of the Ephesians were called Sisyrbitae after Sisyrbe." Strabo, *Geogr.* 14.1.4. See also 11.5.4; 12.3.21
11. Strabo, *Geogr.* 14.1.5; Pausanias, *Descr.* 4.31.8.
12. See also Pausanias, *Descr.* 4.31.8.

2. EPHESIAN HISTORY

warriors, who took control of the city. Amazons were so committed to martial arts[13] that they removed their right breasts, which would otherwise impede their javelin throwing.[14] It was said that after its capture, the Amazon leader Hippolyte set up the statue of Artemis and started an annual dance around the city with weapons and shields.[15] The Amazons, the equal of men,[16] would in turn be driven away by the Greek founders.[17]

The earliest accounts are a mixture of plausible history and fable. Strabo, quoting Pherecydes, says that the area was first occupied by Carians[18] who Herodotus describes as being Minoans.[19] These inhabitants were driven out by the Ionians led by Androclus, the legitimate son of Cordus, the last king of Athens ca. 1068 BC, giving the city royal prestige.[20] His descendants still had royal honors in Paul's time.[21] There was the belief that Apollo had directed the location for the founding of the city leading them through muses,[22] who took the shape of bees.[23] Androclus was given a vision that he was to establish a city where he found a fish and a boar. When the Greeks landed at Ephesus harbor a boar broke cover, and Androclus chased it and killed it.[24] The story of Androclus can still be seen on a frieze in the temple of Hadrian.

13. Strabo, *Geogr.* 11.5.3.

14. Amazons were named after this practice. *Amaza* in Greek means breastless. McDonald, "Ephesus," 318.

15. McDonald, "Ephesus," 318.

16. Homer, *Iliad* 3.189; 6.186.

17. Pausanias, *Descr.* 4.31.8; 7.2.6–9.

18. Strabo, *Geogr.* 14.1.3.

19. Herodotus, *Hist.* 1.171.1–3.

20. Strabo, *Geogr.* 14.1.3; Pausanias, *Descr.* 7.2.7–8.

21. Strabo, *Geogr.* 14.1.3.

22. In Ancient Greek religion, the Nine Muses were the sons and daughters of Zeus and Mnemosyne (the personification of memory) and were seen as the personification of knowledge and the arts.

23. Philostratus, *Imag.* 2.8.

24. Athenaeus, *Deipn.* 8.62.

EPHESUS: THE NURSERY OF CHRISTIANITY

Temple of Hadrian

Pausanias records the death of Androclus in battle with the people of Priene against the Carians.[25] An elaborate heroon[26] with similar artwork has also been identified.[27] These varying stories, some totally myth and some a mixture of history and myth entered deeply into the religious consciousness of the Ephesians.

Ephesian History

While the religious setting will be the main area of interest for most readers, this did not happen in a vacuum. An emphasis of this book is the intertwined religious and political landscape in Ephesus following Alexander, and how that eventually provided the setting for many of the books of the New Testament. To get that destination it is necessary to trawl through a relatively dry list of dates and names of generals and battles. I will start by briefly outline what is known

---

25. Pausanias, *Descr.* 7.2.8–9.
26. A cenotaph or funerary monument.
27. Thür, "Processional Way," 172.

2. EPHESIAN HISTORY

of the city's earliest history. The twelve Ionian cities, called the Panionic League, were established on the west coast of Anatolia by ca. 750 BC. The Lydian[28] kings attacked the area and ruled over several cities including Ephesus in the sixth and seventh centuries.[29] Ephesus would eventually be besieged by Croesus ca. 550 BC, but despite his harsh treatment of the Ionians, he was the main benefactor in the construction of the first large temple of Artemis.[30] During this time of Lydian supremacy the population became more mixed than in any other city in the league.[31]

Croesus, the last of the Lydian kings, was defeated by the Persian, Cyrus, bringing Ephesus under Persian rule till 480 BC, at which time the armies of Greece defeated the Persians at the sea battle of Salamis. The city then became part of an alliance of Greek city states called the Delian league[32] and in 466 BC, Ephesus then came under the control of Athens.[33] During the Peloponnesian war in 412 BC, Ephesus sided with Sparta[34] and then reverted to the Persians at the beginning of the fourth century. The city had enjoyed better relations with Persia than the other Ionian cities but, generally, instability marked its political life from the defeat of the Persians at Salamis through to Lysimachus's reign (ca. 290 BC.)[35] The Persians in turn were defeated by Alexander the Great in 334 BC. Ephesus was taken by Alexander without a fight, and he restored all the taxes paid by the temple of Artemis to Persia and restored its democratic leaders.[36] Also this reduced the instability that had gone back forty-two years previously to his father, Philip's, time[37] and by reintroducing democracy was a way of continuing

28. Lydia comprised the western region of Asia Minor.
29. McDonald, "Ephesus," 318.
30. Oster, "Ephesus," 543.
31. Oster, "Ephesus," 543.
32. Arnold, "Ephesus," 249.
33. McDonald, "Ephesus," 319.
34. Arnold, "Ephesus," 249.
35. Oster, "Ephesus," 543.
36. Arrian, *Anab.* 1.18.
37. Fox, *Alexander the Great*, 117. Thrace is the region in Southeast

EPHESUS: THE NURSERY OF CHRISTIANITY

the support of the Greek cities of Asia. For Ephesus, this democracy was one dominated by Macedonian loyalists.[38]

Alexander died unexpectedly in 323 BC, and without an appointed successor, there commenced what he had predicted, the "funeral games,"[39] where his generals fought over the pickings of his short-lived empire. Because of its strategic and commercial importance Ephesus would become a focus of attention of these former generals and the fortunes of war would have a massive impact on the future history of the city. It would also fundamentally change the way Artemis was worshiped and how successive rulers would view themselves. For these reasons, this period must be dealt with in more detail than others.

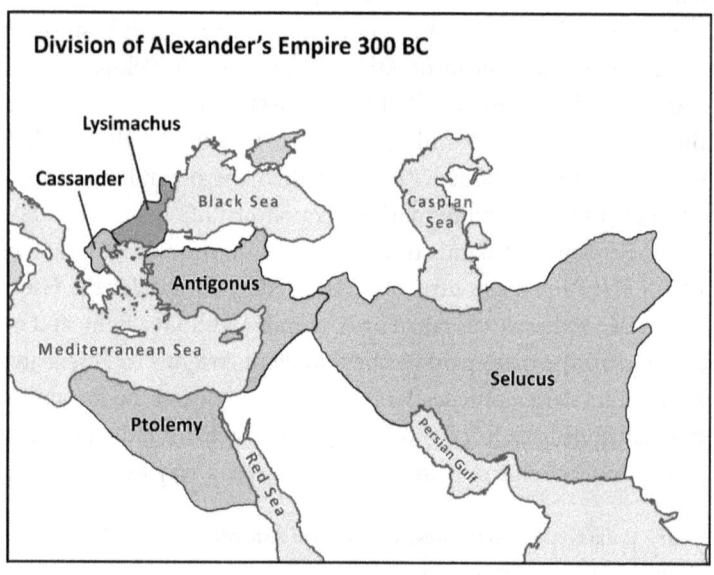

Division of Alexander's empire by his generals in 303 BC

Europe, now split among Bulgaria, Greece, and Turkey, which is bounded by the Balkan Mountains to the north, the Aegean Sea to the south, and the Black Sea to the east.

38. Rogers, *Mysteries of Artemis*, 48.
39. Arrian, *Anab.* 7.26.3.

2. EPHESIAN HISTORY

Cassander, became king of Macedonia, Antigonus ruled in Asia, Lysimachus was given Thrace,[40] Ptolemy had taken Egypt and proclaimed himself Pharoah and Seleucus ruled in what was called the upper satrapies.[41] Cassander became concerned about the growing power of his neighbor, Greece, whose hostile actions had been directed towards him, so he sent an envoy to Antigonus in Asia asking him to come to terms with him. The only terms he would accept was for Cassander to surrender all his territory to him. This would prove a very fateful decision. Cassander then approached Lysimachus in neighboring Thrace, and in turn, he then sent embassies to Ptolemy and Seleucus who agreed to join the war with Antigonus. They saw the belligerence of Antigonus as a threat to all their kingdoms.[42]

---

40. Fox, *Alexander the Great*, 474.

41. Diodorus, *Historical*, 20.106.1–5. The "upper satrapies" refers to that part of Alexander's empire that was east of the river Tigris.

42. Diodorus, *Historical*, 20.106.1–5.

EPHESUS: THE NURSERY OF CHRISTIANITY

Portrait head of Lysimachus from the Ephesus Museum

Lysimachus's general, Prepelaos, frightened Ephesus into capitulation in 302 BC. He apparently left Ephesus a "free" city, a word that they defined for their own self-interest.[43] How free it was is questionable as an embassy had to be sent to Prepelaos in 302 BC to gain tax-free status for Artemis so her temple was not looted

43. Rogers, *Mysteries of Artemis*, 53.

2. EPHESIAN HISTORY

and to prevent troops being billeted in her sanctuary.[44] Prepelaos burned all the ships in the harbors as Antigonus, his enemy controlled the sea, and the outcome of the war was very uncertain.[45] Antigonus then ordered his son Demetrios Poliorcetes (Destroyer of Cities) to stop fighting Kassandra and come to terms with him which in turn allowed Demetrios to sail into Ephesus with his whole army causing Prepelaos to withdraw.[46] Part of the agreement with Kassandra was that the Greek cities in Ionia were to be free[47] and he returned Ephesus to its former state as a democracy.[48] In this conflict Ephesus would choose the wrong side which would lead to the destruction of the classical city.

Antigonus was killed in battle against Prepelaos in 301 BC[49] after which his kingdom was divided among the victors which included giving Asia Minor to Lysimachus. In reality, Ephesus was hard to capture, and it remained under the control of Demetrios for a further eight years. Epigraphical propaganda that justified Demetrios's struggle against Lysimachus was created with the involvement and apparent active role of both those parties that ran the Artemision as well as the city administration.[50] Grants of citizenship to those who assisted in the struggle were inscribed on the walls of the Artemision making the sanctuary itself part of the propaganda.[51] It appears that Lysimachus cut the city off from the fertile plains nearby causing considerable damage to the estates of Ephesian citizens.[52] However, Demetrios's navy controlled the

---

44. Rogers, *Mysteries of Artemis*, 47. The city may have been free to determine its internal affairs.

45. Diodorus, *Historical*, 20.107.4.

46. Diodorus, *Historical*, 20.111.3.

47. Diodorus, *Historical*, 20.111.2.

48. Diodorus, *Historical*, 20.111.3.

49. Plutarch, *Demedtr.* 18–19.

50. Rogers, *Mysteries of Artemis*, 44–51, 55. This conclusion is in part based on the decree of Ephesian citizenship for a certain Apollonides who obtained favourable terms from Demetrios.

51. Rogers, *Mysteries of Artemis*, 57.

52. Rogers, *Mysteries of Artemis*, 55–58.

harbor and supplied it by sea. To get assistance against this navy, Lysimachus mended a dispute he had with Ptolemy I Soter and sealed the alliance by marrying his sister Arsinoe and in response Seleucus aligned with Demetrios for a time.

There are different accounts of how Lysimachus took Ephesus, which may have happened in 294 BC though these all involve subterfuge and a pirate chief.[53] But that was not the end of the matter. Demetrios was building a large fleet and planned to take the land in Asia held formerly by his father Antigonus, meaning Ephesus was vulnerable to assault by sea. The years of conflict had shown that the low-lying classical city centered south and east of the Artemision would have been impossible to hold without control of the sea.[54] Big changes had to be made to secure Ephesus. There also had to be a reckoning for the city and for Artemis's support of Demetrios and Lysimachus's response would show his reputation for opportunism and ruthlessness.[55] His punishment was thorough as it involved both the rearrangement of Ephesus itself and its religious ties with the temple.[56] The siting of the classical city around the Artemision meant there was an unavoidably strong link between the town and the temple. For all its renown and military significance, the original harbor of Croesus, known as the "sacred harbor"[57] had become silted and, as mentioned under *Geography*, the setting was at best generally pestilential.

Lysimachus's answer was to build a totally new city around the higher ground and also a new harbor. This is the city of the New Testament writers. He named the city Arsinoeia after his wife and the sister of his ally, Ptolemy. This was not an expansion of and a renaming of an existing city but the construction of an entirely new city. Arsinoeia was built between the hills Bulbul Dagh and Panayir Dagh over an old cemetery. A large city wall, nine kilometers long, seven meters high, and three meters thick along with

---

53. Polyaenus, *Strat.* 5.19; Frontinus, *Strat.* 3.3.7.
54. Rogers, *Mysteries of Artemis*, 63.
55. Rogers, *Mysteries of Artemis*, 62.
56. Rogers, *Mysteries of Artemis*, 60–61.
57. Athenaeus, *Deipn.* 8.361e.

2. EPHESIAN HISTORY

watchtowers was built to a unified plan over the difficult terrain.[58] The walls enclosed 988 acres, a vast area at the time,[59] and were "the mightiest of all contemporary fortification walls, strong to the point of brutality."[60] It is estimated that 650,000 cubic meters of stone were needed for their construction. Such extensive fortification points to a very unstable world. While we are accustomed to gradual changes in our cities, the "Mediterranean world was often shaped by more abrupt, radical changes—ones that appeared as suddenly as a torrential rainfall, the first tremors of a massive earthquake, or the sight of invaders ships on the horizon."[61] Like the majority of those in the Roman Empire, Ephesians lived only one failed harvest or a locust swarm from starvation.

Strong defenses were not the only consideration when laying out Arsinoeia as it was also architecturally superior to many Greek cities. The layout of the city with its geometrical layout of the agora adjacent to the new harbor showed that the architects followed some principles of a Hippodamian[62] plan. Buildings were grouped and areas of the city set out in a functional relationship with each other.[63] The new layout served the city for 500 years. This plan delivered a community where "assemblies of citizens and public spectacles, competitions, and commerce [would be] conducted communally in public . . . with soldiers, citizens and traders interacting with each other."[64] The designers made use of a winding valley that exploited the terrain for visual effect. The neighboring towns of Lebedos and Kolophon were destroyed, and their residents moved to Arsinoeia to help populate it.[65] The result

---

58. Strabo, *Geogr.* 14.1.21; Rogers, *Mysteries of Artemis*, 67.

59. Rogers, *Mysteries of Artemis*, 68. Priene, another of the rebuilt and planned Ionian cities, only covered ninety-one acres.

60. Rogers, *Mysteries of Artemis*, 68.

61. Rogers, *Mysteries of Artemis*, 275.

62. Named after Hippodamus of Miletus who developed town planning based on a grid-like pattern.

63. Rogers, *Mysteries of Artemis*, 70.

64. Rogers, *Mysteries of Artemis*, 70–71.

65. While ruthless, this action was not unique in the Hellenistic world at

was a forced synchronism of three presumably unhappy groups without a common connection, but the architecture was intended to help counter that. However, democracy was gone, and it was replaced effectively with the rule of one man, Lysimachus.[66]

The citizens of classical Ephesus were reluctant to move[67] from the old city which meant being separated from their Artemision. According to the story recorded by Strabo, the king flooded the streets of the old city by blocking the sewers so forcing the move.[68] It is suggested though, that he may have been fed anti-Lysimachus rhetoric as there is a different account of the move. Duris of Elaea (born ca. 350 BC) claims that a flood washed away "countless dwellings and the wealth of many prosperous years."[69] It is just as likely that the old city, built on a flood plain, was washed into the sea. This would have been fortuitous for Lysimachus but as Durius said, it left the inhabitants wondering where their saving gods were.[70] For Lysimachus there was no doubt. Artemis had been the "savior" of he and his followers and had delivered them in their military struggles and he now would worship her in her mysteries.[71]

With the population separated from the Artemision by a swamp and not easy to access all year round this would have reduced the authority of the priests and priestesses. By making this physical separation, "he created an interwoven structure of political and religious authority outside the Artemision and its administration. Against the will of the Ephesians, Lysimachus helped to liberate the Ephesians, and even Artemis herself, from the authority of the Artemision."[72] The priests and priestesses lost the time.

66. Rogers, *Mysteries of Artemis*, 74, 76.

67. Possibly because the new city was on top of a cemetery. Knibbe, "Via Sacra," 144.

68. Strabo, *Geogr.* 14.1.21.

69. Duris, *Anth. Gr.* 9.424.

70. Duris, *Anth. Gr.* 9.424,

71. Rogers, *Mysteries of Artemis*, 76–80.

72. Rogers, *Mysteries of Artemis*, 87.

2. EPHESIAN HISTORY

the ability to decide how Artemis was to be worshiped during the annual celebrations of her birth. Nor could they decide what her nature was as a goddess"[73] Lysimachus removed the mysteries of Artemis from the control of the priests and priestesses of the Artemision and "made the celebration of Artemis's mysteries into a cult of salvation managed by the polis."[74] He built a new temple and statue to the savior at Ortygia, about five hours' walk from the city center where mysteries and sacrifices were performed.[75] This is presumably one of the newer temples referred to by Strabo where there was already a famous statue of the mother and nurse of Artemis.[76] By his actions, Lysimachus turned Arsinoeia into a "'bipolar city'—a polis with two sanctuaries for the worship of Artemis."[77] He would not be the last ruler to define who was the savior and dictate how that savior was to be worshiped. These changes are examined further in the section "Ephesian Religion." Coinage issued at the time shows an image of Arsinoe and on the reverse a quiver, bow, and arrow, the symbols of Artemis suggesting an assimilation of the queen with the goddess.[78]

There was another change of alliances and Lysimachus was killed in 281 BC at the battle of Corupedium, fighting against a Seleucid-Ptolemaic coalition. This would be the final battle of Alexanders successors. Arsinoe escaped the city bearing her name and with her gone, the city changed its name back to Ephesus. That was not the end of Arsinoe, however, as she went to Egypt where, in ca. 274 BC, she married her full brother Ptolemy II despite all he had done to destroy the work of her husband. She took on the role of queen and co ruled with her brother who had her proclaimed

73. Rogers, *Mysteries of Artemis*, 85.
74. Rogers, *Mysteries of Artemis*, 61.
75. Rogers, *Mysteries of Artemis*, 75–88. His conclusion is drawn in part from an inscription commemorating the foundation of the city and the establishment of a new temple and image and a grant to enable the members of the sunhedrion of the Gerousia (council of elders) to feast and sacrifice at the mysteries and sacrifices of the saviour goddess.
76. Strabo, *Geogr.* 14.1.20.
77. Rogers, *Mysteries of Artemis*, 88.
78. Brenk, "Artemis," 158–9.

as a god and ensured she was worshiped. Her role as a ruler was unprecedented and opened the way for later Ptolemaic queens, Cleopatra being the most famous.

The city had already come under Egyptian control in 309 BC and was then ruled by Ptolemy I Soter. The city changed hands a number of times, as we have seen, but kept reverting to Ptolemaic rule with an Egyptian garrison present as late as 221 BC.[79] Antiochus III,[80] driven by the city's strategic importance, seized the city in 197 BC.[81]

Ephesus was then in turn ruled by the Greeks until 133 BC when Attalus III of Pergamum willed his kingdom to the Romans. The Romans made Ephesus the capital of the province of Asia, removing the title from Pergamum.[82] It would be many years before the city's relation with Rome would be settled and there would come periods of control by the Seleucids and Ptolemies.

Ephesus paid dearly for collaborating with Mithridates VI,[83] king of Pontus during the First Mithridatic War (89–85 BC). He was seen as a deliverer because of the harshness of Roman rule.[84] In this insurrection 80,000 Romans were killed on one day. Appian wrote of the horrors of possibly the first genocide which is known as the "Asiatic vespers" or the "Ephesian vespers" and occurred in 88 BC, saying:

> [Mithridates] wrote secretly to all his satraps and magistrates that on the thirtieth day thereafter they should set upon all Romans and Italians in their towns, and upon their wives and children and their domestics of Italian birth, kill them and throw their bodies out unburied, and share their goods with himself. He threatened to punish any who should bury the dead or conceal the living and

---

79. Polybius, *Histories*, 5.35.2.

80. The father of Antiochus IV Epiphanes (god manifest) (ca. 215 to 164 BC) who persecuted the devout Jews in Judea.

81. Walters, "Egyptian Religions," 286.

82. McDonald, "Ephesus," 318.

83. Mithridates VI, one of Rome's most formidable enemies, was finally defeated by Pompey in the Third Mithridatic War of 75 to 65 BC.

84. Arnold, "Ephesus," 249.

2. EPHESIAN HISTORY

offered rewards to informers and to those who should kill persons in hiding, and freedom to slaves for betraying their masters. To debtors for killing money-lenders he offered release from one half of their obligations. These secret orders Mithridates sent to all the cities at the same time. When the appointed day came calamities of various kinds befell the province of Asia.[85]

Appian's account continues in harrowing detail of the butchery that ensued in the different cities including in the sanctuary of the Artemisium.

Instead of proving to be the hoped-for deliverer, Mithridates oppression was far worse than that of the Romans! After the city was taken again at the end of the war, the Roman consul Lucius Cornelius Sulla forced the immediate payment of five years taxation, the expenses of the war, and other associated costs. Appian describes the calamity saying, "The cities, oppressed by poverty, borrowed it at high rates of interest and mortgaged their theatres, their gymnasiums, their walls, their harbors, and every other scrap of public property."[86] After collecting the money, Sulla sailed back to Rome and left Asia to the mercy of fleets of pirates which had been set up by Mithridates to aid him in his war. And so, "the province of Asia had her fill of misery."[87]

During the time of the Roman republic[88] there was veneration of Dea Roma and certain Roman officials.[89] At the end of the republic, the city was also involved with the troubles in Italy and Anthony and Cleopatra were received in the winter of 33–32 BC. Unfortunately for Ephesus, Anthony was on his way to defeat at Actium and the city again suffered for supporting the loser.

---

85. Appian, *Mith.* 4.22.
86. Appian, *Mith.* 9.62–3.
87. Appian, *Mith.* 9.63.
88. The Roman republic started when the monarch was removed in 510 BC and became the Roman empire after the autocratic rule of the Caesars was established 41–27 BC.
89. Oster, "Ephesus," 543.

EPHESUS: THE NURSERY OF CHRISTIANITY

Under Augustus came stability, especially through his claim that he "restored peace to the sea from pirates,"[90] which led to prosperity and the city's prominence for 200 years.[91] Irenaeus[92] said of this time "through their [the Romans] instrumentality the world is at peace, and we walk on the highways without fear, and sail where we will."[93] However, Augustus, the adopted son of the god Julius Caesar, made the leap from doing the work of god to being a god himself.[94] Ephesus not only continued as the capital of the province of Asia but enjoyed a building boom which revitalized the city. Strabo said it "grows daily and is the largest emporium in Asia."[95] Essential infrastructure that was needed for a growing city such as the construction of aqueducts and repaving streets was undertaken[96] but also buildings that reinforced the city's political importance. This included triumphal monuments to prominent Romans and the "comprehensive Romanization of the civic space."[97] This Romanization included a new large political center called the state agora (58 meters by 160 meters) surrounded by a number of temples (Roma and Julius Caesar, Flavians [or Domitians] and Augustus) along with the royal basilica. Also incorporated were pre-Roman governmental institutions, the prytaneion[98]

90. Augustus, *Anc.* 25.

91. Arnold, "Ephesus," 249.

92. Irenaeus, because of his association with Polycarp, is thought to have come from Smyrna near Ephesus in the mid-second century. His comments and others show there was substance to Augustus's imperial propaganda in his *Res Gestae* 25.

93. Irenaeus, *Haer.* 4.30.3.

94. As the adopted son of Julius Caesar, Augustus was termed the son of a god in Rome and was not worshiped as a God by the citizens but allowed himself to be worshiped by non-citizens and this was strongest in the east. Cassius Dio, *Hist. rom.* 51.20.6–8. He was proclaimed a god after his death in AD 14 and joined the Roman pantheon of gods.

95. Strabo, *Geogr.* 14.1.24.

96. Oster, "Ephesus," 543.

97. Oster, "Ephesus," 543.

98. The council chamber which held the holy flame on the hestia (hearth). It was used for "various ceremonies, banquets and receptions for official guests of the city." Arnold, "Ephesus," 249.

2. EPHESIAN HISTORY

and bouleuterion.[99] The cults of Augustus and Artemis were probably celebrated in these.

Due to high mortality and inadequate fertility rates,[100] it was difficult for Roman cities to maintain their population let alone grow.[101] Despite this, under Roman rule the population of Ephesus grew sharply. Philostratus (ca. 170–247) wrote that "all men are carried there as to their native land, and no one is so senseless and inclined to deny the obvious that the city is the common treasury of Asia and her resource [when] in need, and no one is so carping as to criticize the city's expanse."[102] Migration of about 1000 per year was needed just to maintain the city size and about another 1500–1800 needed to allow the city to grow from 100,000 to 200,000 over a century. Native residents would have quickly been outnumbered. Estimates place the number of outsiders exceeding locals at somewhere between thirty-three to fifty years. The broad multicultural nature of the city can be seen in the number of different gods worshiped. The tension that existed between foreigners and locals can also be perceived in Acts 18:24—19:41. Despite this influx, the city would remain viewed as "a Greek polis, a haven of Greek identity."[103]

At the end of the first century AD Ephesus presented itself "as first and greatest metropolis of Asia" in numerous inscriptions and its coins.[104] It has been described as the leading city of

---

99. Oster, "Ephesus," 543–44. The senate house used by the *boule*, the advisory council of the city.

100. It has been estimated that the net population growth in the Roman world was -0.5 percent PA. Infant mortality has been assessed at 33 percent in the first year. White, "Urban Development," 45–46.

101. White, "Urban Development," 45.

102. Philostratus, *Vit. Soph.* 1.23

103. Thomas, "At Home," 83. This claim is based on the picture painted of Ephesus in the two remaining Greek novels of the Roman period that are centred around Ephesus, *Ephesiaka* by Xenophon and Achilles Tatius's story of *Leucippe and Clitophon*. This may have been more perception than reality.

104. White, "Urban Development," 34.

EPHESUS: THE NURSERY OF CHRISTIANITY

the richest region of the Roman empire.[105] Aelius Aristides[106] also spoke of Ephesus being the most prosperous commercial center of his time in Asia, controlling the affairs of the whole region. Roman milestones to cities in Asia were based on Ephesus.[107] Philostratus, writing after the beginning of the second century but claiming to quote Apollonius of Tyana[108] in a first-century setting, described Ephesus as:

> a city which took the basis of its race from the purest Attic source, and which grew in size beyond all other cities of Ionia and Lydia, and stretched herself out to the sea outgrowing the land on which she is built, and is filled with studious people, both philosophers and rhetoricians, thanks to whom the city owes her strength, not to her cavalry, but to the tens of thousands of her inhabitants in whom she encourages wisdom.[109]

A serious earthquake struck Ephesus in AD 23. Buildings on the lower slope of Bubul Dagh (refer to pages 26 and 27) were destroyed and much of the cleared space was set aside for public buildings. The largest project was the new Tetragonos (or four-cornered) Agora, the commercial center built around a 112-meter square with an open courtyard.[110]

---

105. Arnold, "Ephesus," 249.

106. Aelius Aristides, *Orat.* 23.24. Aelius Aristides (AD 117–81) was a popular orator during the Roman Empire. His work has incidental value in showing social life in Asia Minor in the second century.

107. Arnold, "Ephesus," 249.

108. Apollonius, from the south of modern Turkey, lived in the first century AD and was a teacher and alleged miracle worker. He received divine honours in the third century.

109. Philostratus, *Vit. Apoll.* 8.7.8.

110. Scherrer, "City of Ephesos," 8.

2. EPHESIAN HISTORY

View of the commercial agora

The theater at Ephesus

EPHESUS: THE NURSERY OF CHRISTIANITY

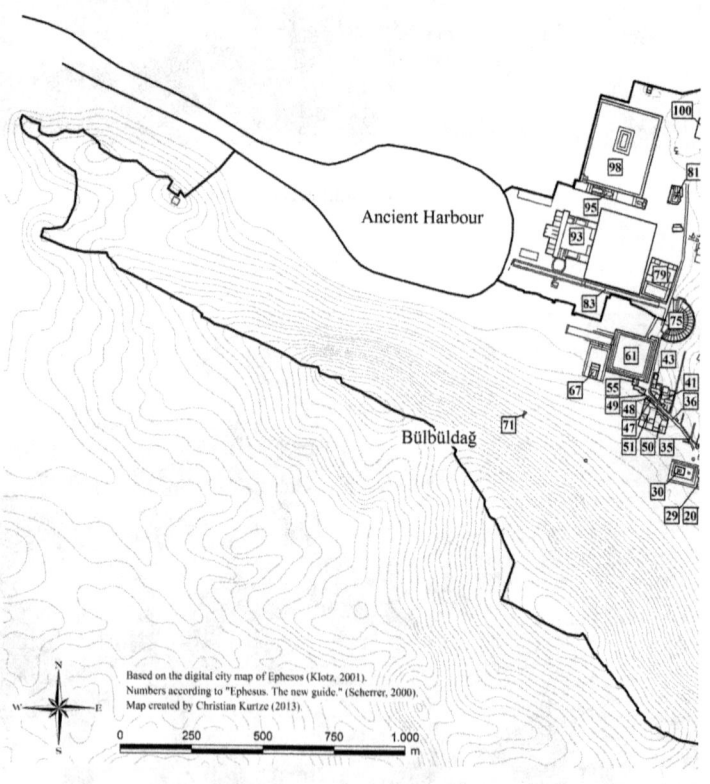

2. EPHESIAN HISTORY

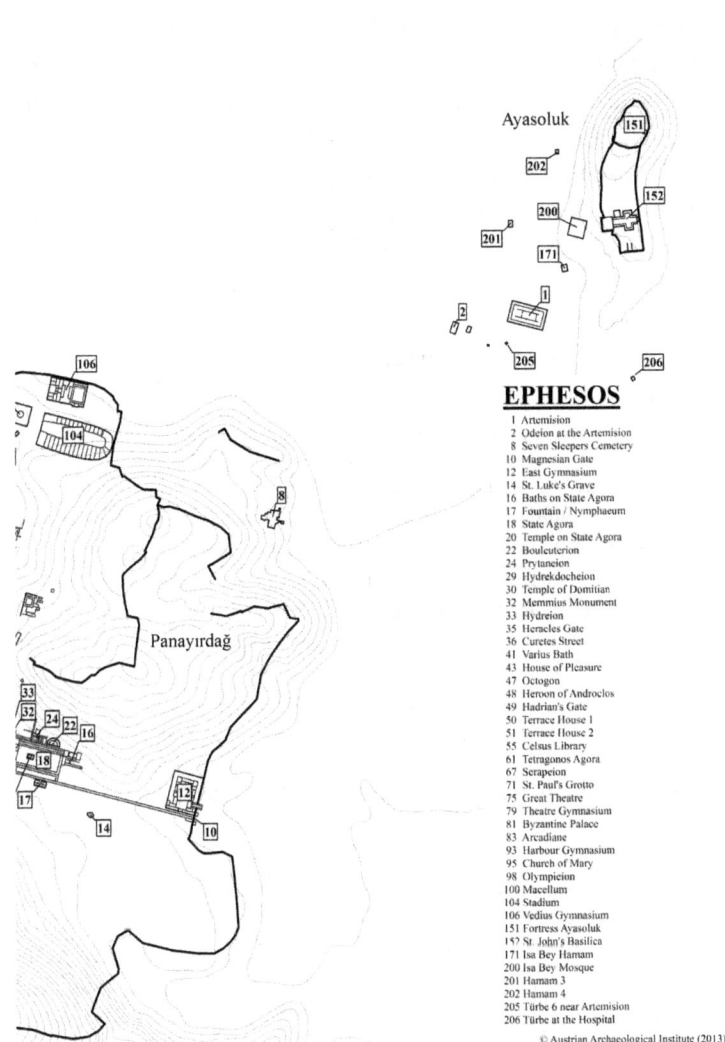

Layout of Ephesus during the Roman period showing the harbor

EPHESUS: THE NURSERY OF CHRISTIANITY

During Nero's reign the theater was extended, the stadium reconstructed, and a second story built to the Tetragonos Agora. The city's basic layout dated to the Augustine period but the bulk of the building, in volume and quality, dates from the Flavians (AD 69–96) and Antonines (AD 96–192.)[111] Public work during this time was mainly through local benefactors.[112] The city received its first *neokorate*[113] during the Flavian period and also water from the Marnus and Klaseas Rivers and from Tire, a distance of 32 kilometers, was piped to the city.[114] Roads between the major cities were improved which further increased urban prosperity and population mobility.[115] During this period also, as a display of its wealth and pride, Ephesus decorated itself with high quality architecture, inscriptions and statues.

The city with its surrounding areas grew to about 200–250,000[116] and during Paul's time the city may well have been

---

111. White, "Urban Development," 54. The Flavians cover the rule from Vespasian to Domitian while the Antonines went from Nerva to Commodus and these are sometimes called the Five Good Emperors.

112. From Hadrian to the early Antonine period Asian and Greek benefactors could be promoted to public office and even the Senate. This gave them acceptance and allowed them to move beyond their social setting. White, "Urban Development," 56, 63.

113. The term was used for an official who had responsibility "related to the precincts of a deity. During the Roman imperial period, however, 'neokoros' took on a specialized meaning. It became the technical term for a city where a provincial temple of the emperors was located." Friesen, "Roman Emperors," 229.

114. Scherrer, "City of Ephesos," 9. This pipeline, like many of the public structures in Ephesus, was donated by a private citizen, speaking of the extreme wealth accumulated by some.

115. White, "Urban Development," 54. The largely unpaved Persian roads were replaced by a standardized Roman pattern: "as a rule they measure about eight metres wide; each side was stabilized by a row of magines, rectangular blocks measuring up to sixty centimeters along the sides, which contained a surface of packed cobbles sloping gently down on either side from a central spina." Mitchell, *Anatolia I*, 125–26.

116. Calculating population figures is virtually impossible. Figures quoted go as low as 51,000 up to 250,000. There were known to be 40,000 citizens in the third century, and to that had to be added women, children and slaves. White, "Urban Development," 42.

2. EPHESIAN HISTORY

at its zenith.[117] But for a few cities, this is a population far exceeding anything found in Europe till modern time. It has been said that "it was probably the third largest city in the east behind Alexandria and Antioch on the Orontes (Syria) but its place in prominence was third behind Rome and Alexandria."[118] Ephesus had continuing problems with silting of its harbor. Strabo describes this silting as going back to the Greek period and that attempts were made to control this by building a mole at the river mouth.[119] Despite the later Roman harbor basin not being deep it could accommodate large cargo ships 30 meters long and of approximately 400–500 gross register tons.[120]

Gymnasiums had always been very important in Greek culture. After the conquest of Greece, the cities of Asia Minor became a refuge for Hellenism and the Greek athletic tradition.[121] Six of these are known to have existed in Ephesus in the mid second century.[122] The largest was an open space called the *Xystoi* (commenced ca. AD 92)[123] measuring 200 by 240 meters and was built on drained ground. It was surrounded by a three-aisled portico on each side (thus giving its name) and may have been used to host the Olympic Games.[124] The city had become monumental in its access and appearance. Much of this construction allowed large numbers to participate in festivals and processions associated with the worship of the emperor.[125] This construction dominated the

117. Edward Blaiklock says the city was in decline. Blaiklock, "Ephesus," 181. This is contrary to Oster's assessment. Oster, "Ephesus," 543. Strabo's contemporary assessment seems clear.

118. McDonald, "Ephesus," 319.

119. Strabo, *Geogr.* 14.1.24.

120. This claim is based on the dimensions of an antique wreck found at Pantano Longarini in Sicily. Zabehlicky, *Preliminary Views*, 209. A register ton is 100 cubic feet or 2.8 cubic meters.

121. Arnold, *Festivals of Ephesus*, 17.

122. Scherrer, "City of Ephesos," 14.

123. Refer to section *The Imperial Cult* for the significance of this and the associated buildings.

124. Scherrer, "City of Ephesos," 13.

125. Van der Linde, "Artemis Ephesia," 170–71.

harbor which meant that all visitors "could not miss this expression of imperial grandeur and divinity."[126]

Ephesus underwent an unprecedented building boom during the middle of the second century[127] and the city prospered up to the late second century. It was ravaged by a short but severe plague bought back by Roman troops in AD 166 which may also have been associated with a famine.[128] Major construction funded by private donations, a key factor in the continual renewal and growth of the city virtually dried up around this time till another great benefactor was found during the reign of Severus Alexander (AD 222–35). He built, among other things, halls for the different corporations of artisans. The city would have to wait a century for another similar benefactor.[129]

More damaging to Ephesus was the deterioration of the eastern border of the empire caused by the incompetence and cruelty of the Roman rulers in the late second and third centuries. Problems facing the city and the whole of Anatolia were the "depletion of political and administrative leaders through assignations, aggressive pogroms against Christians, and the increase of foreign intervention from Parthians in Mesopotamia and from Goths in Russia."[130] Large construction work continued but the city, including the great temple of Artemis, was severely damaged by a number of seaborne attacks by the Goths ending centuries without destructive invasion.[131] It had been thought that the city declined in late antiquity but that was not substantiated by the archaeological record. It would be continually renewed, changing from a "Hellenistic Roman metropolis to a Byzantine–Christian center."[132] During the

---

126. Van der Linde, "Artemis Ephesia," 172.
127. White, "Urban Development," 30.
128. Rogers, *Mysteries of Artemis*, 170.
129. Scherrer, "City of Ephesos," 14–15.
130. Oster, "Ephesus," 544.
131. Oster, "Ephesus," 544,
132. Scherrer, "City of Ephesos," 25.

time of transition and crisis from Roman rule the city continued to prosper unlike other cities such as Corinth.[133]

Roman era aqueduct

During the time of Valentinian (reigned AD 364–75) there was little building; the effect on Ephesus was worsened by earthquakes every couple of years. Construction resumed under Theodosius I (reigned AD 379–95) who was regarded as the new founder of the city.[134] There were severe earthquakes again in the fourth century which caused extensive damage to the whole area

133. Scherrer, "City of Ephesos," 29.
134. Scherrer, "City of Ephesos," 21.

and Lysimachus's city was largely deserted. The city divided into two, with one center around the harbor within a reduced walled area and the other on the hill of Ayasoluk.[135] Large-scale construction and renovations continued through to the fourth century[136] despite a number of earthquakes. Destroyed buildings, such as the state agora, served as quarries for new ones and other items such as columns and relief panels were recycled.[137] Restoration of the water supply and baths was a major concern.[138] Up to the end of the fourth century Ephesus would still call itself "the first and greatest metropolis of Asia."[139]

After ca. 350, the inscriptions honoring the emperors were written so as not to offend Christians and major Christian buildings were being constructed.[140] Most of the twenty churches[141] known in Ephesus date before the Council of Ephesus in AD 431.[142] Imperial edicts in AD 391 and 392 forbade the pagan cults and Ephesus was able to construct officially condoned churches through utilizing stone taken from the old sacred buildings.[143] It appears little changed in Ephesus between the fourth and fifth centuries and the city is known to be flourishing in AD 616.[144]

Ephesian Archaeology

The first serious archaeological expedition was undertaken from 1863–74 by John T. Wood who was commissioned by the British

135. Oster, "Ephesus," 544.
136. Scherrer, "City of Ephesos," 15.
137. Scherrer, "City of Ephesos," 19.
138. Scherrer, "City of Ephesos," 18.
139. White, "Urban Development," 34.
140. Scherrer, "City of Ephesos," 18–19.
141. But for two, these were small and scattered throughout the city suggesting they served different neighborhoods. White, "Urban Development," 23.
142. Scherrer, "City of Ephesos," 25.
143. Scherrer, "City of Ephesos," 18–19.
144. White, "Urban Development," 34.

2. EPHESIAN HISTORY

Museum to find the temple of Artemis.[145] Fortunately he was able to find an inscription describing the route to the great temple. By following this route, he eventually discovered the temple under 6 meters of topsoil![146] But for a brief return to the site in 1904–5, the association with the British Museum ceased however, a base from one of the great temple's pillars is on display in the museum.

But for the breaks between the two wars, permission to excavate Ephesus has rested with the Austrian Archaeological Institute since 1893. This has meant that much of the results has not been available to the English reader. While this work has been extensive, it is estimated that only 10 percent of the city has been excavated.[147] As large areas are in private ownership with fruit plantations, actual excavation requires special permits, but non-invasive geophysical surveys have been undertaken.[148] Despite this, their work has been described as one of the great gifts of the last century.[149] The city can be visited by up to two million people a year which helps fund ongoing research and excavation. With the aid of reconstructions, such as the Library of Celsus and the open-air theater, tourists can see an ancient city without the intrusion of a modern society.

Ephesus is now the most extensively excavated major city among the eastern Roman Empire and likely the most thoroughly studied.[150] This is allowing researchers to develop an understanding of what was unique about the city as opposed to general Panhellenic traits.[151]

---

145. Oster, "Ephesus," 544.
146. Oster, "Ephesus," 544.
147. "Ephesus," para. 1.
148. Austrian Archaeological Institute, "Ephesos: Periurban Research," para. 1.
149. White, "Urban Development," 27.
150. Rogers, *Mysteries of Ephesus*, 30.
151. Rogers, *Mysteries of Ephesus*, 30.

Inscriptions and Coinage

Many references will be made to inscriptions found in Ephesus, of which thousands have been found. They were generally of high quality and durable and as such were a vital part of the social memory. They were also a way of guiding the discussion and perceptions as residents and visitors walked the streets of the city center.[152] Because the vocabulary was repetitious a person did not need a high degree of literacy to read them.

Coins were more than just a means of enabling commerce. Like inscriptions they were used to mold the Ephesian identity and its relation to its gods and rulers. When coins were first minted in Ephesus in the sixth century BC, Artemis or her symbols were depicted on them, and in the first century AD the Artemision regularly appeared. Her image(s) or symbol(s) continued on coins up to the mid-third century AD. While coinage was used to promote the imperial cult, the presence of Artemis, a different god on the same coin, showed her continuing presence and her relation to the emperor.[153]

---

152. Van der Linde, "Artemis Ephesia," 178.
153. Van der Linde, "Artemis Ephesia," 191–92.

3. Ephesian Freedom

DEMOCRACY, WITH ITS LOVE of freedom, is Greece's gift to the world. In the classical and early Hellenistic period, "a free city had certain inalienable rights, which usually included political autonomy, immunity from taxation or tribute and freedom from foreign garrisons."[1] Greek freedom has also been described very differently, calling it "the habitual freedom to make war or indulge in internecine feuds."[2] But freedom was not for all. Pausanias tells of the conquest of the land by the Greeks and how at the nearby city of Miletus all the men were killed, and the women were married.[3] The Greeks treated the Asiatics like serfs.[4]

For the Greek cities in Ionia, the love of freedom was no less and subjection to the Persians and the Romans was an especially heavy yoke. Fifty years after Alexander, Priene, one of the Ionian cities proclaimed, "There is no greater blessing for Greeks ... than the blessing of freedom."[5] Two centuries of Persian rule went against all this. When Alexander gave the Ionian cities back their freedom he was treated like a god, especially in Ephesus.[6] But the concept of freedom, which would be given lip service by the

---

1. Friesen, "Roman Emperors," 234.
2. Friesen, "Roman Emperors," 237.
3. Pausanias, *Descr.* 7.2.6. Herodotus talks about the difficulty in marrying a woman whose parents you have killed. Herodotus, *Hist.* 1.147.
4. Fox, *Alexander the Great*, 118.
5. Fox, *Alexander the Great*, 118.
6. Strabo, *Geogr.* 14.1.22.

Hellenistic kings, in practice was limited or even ignored.[7] It is fair to say that, "after 334 [BC], while all of the institutions of the classical-era polis of Ephesus continued to function, the informal oligarchization of the polis (that eventually led to a Roman style hierarchization of society following the Roman Conquest) had begun."[8] Even after Demetrios Poliorcetes restored "freedom" to the city in 302 BC it came with the strings of financial obligations, garrisoning, and intervention in the internal affairs of the city.[9] Despite this, compared to other cities, Ephesus was always well-treated by its invaders. It has been said that the city "almost appears to have condescended to be ruled"[10] while at the same time her freedoms were being eroded.

The idea of citizens with equal rights and matching responsibilities was challenged by men who had very different ideas of where power should lie in the city.[11] Freedom, by the first century BC, was no longer the inalienable right but a benevolent grant that a ruler could give or withdraw. In New Testament times, Ephesus was a free city, at least nominally, but the combination of the worship of the powerful city goddess along with the Roman emperor made it firmly a part of Rome's new world order. This really was a return to the situation with the Hellenistic dynasties. The Greeks solved this conflict with their love of freedom by placing the emperor "between human and divine. An intermediate position appropriate to the power of the emperor and the traditions of the Greeks was formed."[12] It was now the emperor who protected their ancient rites.[13]

We perceive the iron rule of Rome from the perspective of accomplished history, but it may not have appeared too secure in the first century as there had been catastrophic civil wars and more

7. Friesen, "Roman Emperors," 243.
8. Rogers, *Mysteries of Artemis*, 49.
9. Rogers, *Mysteries of Artemis*, 53.
10. LiDonnici, "Image of Artemis," 405.
11. Rogers, *Mysteries of Artemis*, 34–35.
12. Friesen, "Roman Emperors," 234.
13. White, "Urban Development," 38.

3. EPHESIAN FREEDOM

would follow after the death of Nero. Until the rule of Vespasian (AD 69–79) it may have been very uncertain where one should place allegiance. Independence became interdependence as commerce grew and transportation links improved and the region, not the individual city, was becoming the important unit.[14] By the late first century there is little if any evidence of resistance to Roman rule and Roman legions were no longer garrisoned in the area.[15] By the second century, Rome had brought nations together and turned them into one city.[16]

Freedom (Latin *libertas*) has as its counterpart peace (Latin *pax*) and these ideas would be part of Roman imperial rhetoric to the time of Constantine. With the unprecedented building boom under Flavian and Antonine emperors (AD 69–212) *libertas* became *liberalitas* (generosity).[17] This bestowing of benefits became the cardinal virtue under Romanization leading to a pluralistic environment especially in the eastern Hellenistic cities.[18] Romanization was an urban phenomenon and limited to the upper levels of society. This process ensured access to Roman skills and resources which led to wealth but for rural Asia Minor it was met with indifference as it had "no compelling social stimuli . . . such as social mobility or wealth."[19]

For all their talk of freedom, Ephesus was one of the major centers of the Roman slave trade[20] and there appears to be little comprehension of its evil. A fanciful *Life of Aesop* (of fable fame) tells of a traveling slave trader who purchases slaves from different regions including Phrygia, Cappadocia, and Lydia and resells them in Ephesus.[21] Being a seaport, Ephesus was ideally suited to

---

14. Friesen, *Twice Neokoros*, 154.
15. Thür, "Processional Way," 164–65.
16. Aelius Aristides, *Orat.* 96.58–61.
17. White, "Urban Development," 30.
18. White, "Urban Development," 30–31.
19. White, "Urban Development," 32.
20. Varro describes how someone might name someone he has purchased in the Ephesian slave market. Varro, *Ling.* 8.21.
21. Koester, "Roman Slave Trade," 778.

transport slaves for the huge market of Rome itself. Two inscriptions, one from the first half of the first century AD and the other from the early second century, refer to the slave market and were written in Latin. The first honors the proconsul in Asia Minor along with the emperor Claudius. And the second a benefactor who gave building projects throughout the city. Using Latin in a Greek-speaking city suggests that there was a group identity among Italian slave traders that made them distinct and "emphasized their special connection with someone important."[22] They were also projecting these important people as being sympathetic to the slave dealers' interests. The presence of these inscriptions show that the traders claimed a legitimate and proper place in Ephesian society.[23]

Not surprisingly, it has been difficult to obtain meaningful information on the inclusion of slaves in society and the religions that flourished in Ephesus. In a religious system that believed their gods loved some more than others, slavery stood testament to this "self-evident" fact. At its worst, slavery in the Roman Empire could exceed the evils of chattel slavery seen in the American south. Gladiatorial contests, the most brutal public expression of the evils of slavery started in Ephesus in 71/70 BC. Slavery at its best could provide a reasonable life (for the time) for someone with sought after skills. A slave's longing for freedom might be worse than slavery itself if it only came when the person was old and/or ill and a burden on his owner. John's vision in Rev 18 when he was in prison on Patmos, not far from Ephesus, pictures the shipping of slaves as a routine part of the commercial life of the city under the power of Rome. Yet what was seen as routine, the sale of human souls (Rev 18:13) was shown in his vision to be subject to the judgement of God. Christianity would welcome slaves as full and valued members where faith, not benefaction, sacrifice, and vows were all that was required. Tradition says that the freed slave Onesimus was the second bishop of Ephesus.

22. Koester, "Roman Slave Trade," 778–79, 780.

23. The inscription to the benefactor Ti Claudius Secundus is matched by an inscription from the Gerousia indicating that they sought a role akin to other associations in the city. Koester, "Roman Slave Trade," 781.

4. Ephesian Artemis

During the long history of Ephesus, it changed from being a Hellenistic city through to a Roman and finally a Byzantine Christian metropolis. The three distinct religious ideologies were not three distinct cultural phases but "an integral process of social change each one building on and through the other . . . in an evolving cultural ecosystem."[1] This chapter explores how the city was owned body, soul, and spirit by the goddess Artemis and the challenges that she posed to Christianity.

Classical Greek Artemis

The Ephesian silversmiths raised a tumult against Paul who had dared to say that gods made by human hands are not gods at all. We are told in Acts 19 that for two hours the citizens of the city shouted, "Great is Artemis of the Ephesians." Despite having the same name, Ephesian Artemis is different in many ways from the Artemis of classical Greece. The meaning of this shared name is uncertain. Some of the suggestions are "'strong limbed' from *artemes*; or 'she who cuts up', since the Spartans called her *Artamis*, from *artao*, or the 'lofty convener', from *airo* and *themis*."[2] Strabo says the goddess' name came from a Greek adjective meaning "safe and sound."[3] Which, if any, of these is correct has been lost in time but it would appear the significance given to the name shifted from

1. White, "Urban Development," 29–31.
2. Graves, *Greek Myths*, 88.
3. Strabo, *Geogr.* 14.1.6.

being a theological statement about her nature to, by Strabo's time, one about her saving benefits for others.

Classical Greek Artemis

In Greek mythology, Artemis was one of the twelve great Olympian gods. She was said to be the daughter of Zeus and Leto, and the twin sister of Apollo.[4] When Artemis was only a child sitting on Zeus's lap, he asked the goddess what gifts he could give her. She asked for eternal virginity, the office of bringing light, a bow and arrows, a hunting tunic, and the company of nine-year-old ocean and river nymphs to care for her hunting hounds.[5] In her images Artemis is pictured armed with a silver bow, standing for the new moon,[6] and she traveled in a golden chariot pulled by two

4. *HH.* 27.
5. Callimachus. *Hymn. Dian.* 1–30.
6. Graves, *Greek Myths*, 87.

4. EPHESIAN ARTEMIS

horned hinds.[7] She is presented as "a traditional tomboy huntress who stood for chastity and the rejection of marriage."[8] Artemis remained a virgin and demanded the same of her assistants.[9] As a virgin she avoided subjugation by a male and was her own master. She appears to have had a strong aversion to anything sexual and so was the complete opposite of Aphrodite.[10] Among the stories reflecting this is a legend that Actaeon[11] watched her as she bathed and to preserve her reputation turned the hapless man into a stag and his own dogs tore him to pieces.[12] As her mother had delivered her without pain, the virgin Artemis became the patroness of childbirth[13] which would seem a paradox to us.

Artemis was held to be a triad—the triple moon goddess. The youngest manifestation was as the maiden of the silver bow. For her principal symbols she had the date palm, a stag, and a bee,[14] and would be served by priestesses aged nine to twelve years.[15] Like her brother, she has the power to kill or to heal humans.[16] Another title given to her was *Mylitta*, the mother of the bee goddess, and, given the Greeks considered honey had almost magical properties to heal, it reinforces the idea that Artemis was seen also as a healing deity.[17] She also took under her sphere the care of mariners.[18]

---

7. Graves, *Greek Myths*, 86.
8. Baugh, "Cult Prostitution," 452.
9. Graves, *Greek Myths*, 87.
10. Hjerrild, "Near Eastern Equivalents," 44.
11. A hero from Thebes in central Greece predating Achilles. Both were trained by the centaur Chiron. Graves, *Greek Myths*, 259.
12. Graves, *Greek Myths*, 87.
13. Callimachus. *Hymn. Dian.* 20–30.
14. Graves, *Greek Myths*, 87.
15. Graves, *Greek Myths*, 87.
16. Graves, *Greek Myths*, 85.
17. Skarmintzo, *Cult of Artemis*, 271.
18. Callimachus, *Hymn. Dian.* 40–45.

Ephesian Artemis

Artemis was held "in honor above all the gods"[19] in Anatolia and there is evidence of her influence spreading not only throughout the Mediterranean but as far as Mesopotamia and Scandinavia.[20] No other city in the Graeco-Roman world belonged body, soul, and spirit to an individual deity as Ephesus did to her.[21] Ephesus and Artemis were inseparably linked to the ancient Greeks.[22] When explaining her prominence Pausanias claimed it arose because of her association with the Amazons who, tradition said, dedicated her image. He added, "Three other points as well have contributed to her renown, the size of the temple, surpassing all buildings among men, the eminence of the city of the Ephesians and the renown of the goddess who dwells there."[23] She offered stability that had stood the test of time[24] and so was able to resist the draw to other gods.

Her rise to prominence over such a vast area (Acts 19:32–35) was not accidental but driven by the missionary zeal of her followers. The goddess was said to be personally involved in spreading her religion by initiating and directing missionary activity and so mirrored Christian missions. The account of the founding of Marseilles (ca. 600 BC) recorded by Strabo illustrates Artemis's involvement with the purposeful spread of her religion:

> They say that when the Phocaeans[25] were about to quit their country, an oracle commanded them to take from Diana of Ephesus a conductor for their voyage. On arriving at Ephesus they therefore inquired how they might

19. Pausanias, *Descr.* 4.31.8.
20. McDonald, "Ephesus," 318.
21. Trebilco, *Early Christians*, 31.
22. There are 524 references to Ephesus on the CD-ROM database *Thesaurus Linguae Graecae*. After deducting the 175 incidental references, one third of the remaining references are associated with the cult of Artemis. Thomas, "At Home," 85.
23. Pausanias, *Descr.* 4.31.8.
24. Strelan, *Paul, Artemis, and the Jews*, 79.
25. Phocaea was another Greek city in Ionia.

4. EPHESIAN ARTEMIS

be able to obtain from the goddess what was enjoined them. The goddess appeared in a dream to Aristarcha, one of the most honorable women of the city, and commanded her to accompany the Phocaeans, and to take with her a plan of the temple and statues. These things being performed, and the colony being settled, the Phocaeans built a temple, and evinced their great respect for Aristarcha by making her priestess. All the colonies [sent out from Marseilles] hold this goddess in peculiar reverence, preserving both the shape of the image [of the goddess], and also every rite observed in the metropolis.[26]

Despite the heights Artemis and her temple reached throughout the Mediterranean and beyond, the goddess had very humble beginnings. It has been suggested that Artemis Ephesia's religious center originated at "a sweet water spring close to the shore and near a sacred tree; this is the origin of Artemis, a tree goddess and a timeless symbol of fertility."[27]

Artemis Ephesia was said to be the mother and ruler of everything,[28] the mistress of the earth's fertility and protector of the dead.[29] Those who called upon her called her "savior," "lord," and "queen of the cosmos."[30] Her main role was as protector and sustainer of the city and its people, like Athens and Athena. One of the goddess' processional routes was around the monuments that remembered the city's history, reinforcing that the goddess acted directly in the affairs of Ephesus.[31] Despite her close association with the city, the association of Ephesian Artemis with the Artemis of classical Greek mythology seems slender. The worship of Ephesian Artemis was a practice described "as far more ancient than their [the Greeks] coming."[32] The form of Artemis worshiped

26. Strabo, *Geogr.* 4.1.4.
27. Knibbe, "Via Sacra," 143.
28. McDonald, "Ephesus," 318.
29. Knibbe, "Via Sacra," 142.
30. Arnold, "Ephesus," 21.
31. LiDonnici, "Image of Artemis," 394.
32. Pausanias, *Descr.* 7.2.6.

in Ephesus was different from that elsewhere in the Greek world which was likely caused by the Greeks assimilating a local earth goddess with their own Artemis. Local mythology relates Artemis Ephesia as a fertile woman born about 7000 BC.[33] The extreme syncretism in this merger makes it difficult to determine which characteristics from the early period are Greek and which are Anatolian. During the Roman period, however, she was brought more in line with Roman and Hellenistic ideas.[34]

Artemis Ephesia

Our clear-cut distinction between religious and secular did not apply in Ephesus, and it would be hard to now find a modern comparison to the relationship between Ephesus and its god. A person belonged to the city and the city belonged to Artemis. She

33. McDonald, "Ephesus," 318.
34. Oster, "Ephesian Artemis," 28.

4. EPHESIAN ARTEMIS

integrated their culture and was the object and source of their devotion. Many coins show an image of Artemis and her temple as these represented Ephesus itself. Harmony in all relationships of life and with the gods came through the practice of *Eusebia*, described by Isocrates as:

> not [destroying] any institution of their fathers and to introduce nothing which was not approved by custom, believing that reverence consists, not in extravagant expenditures, but in disturbing none of the rites which their ancestors had handed on to them. And so also the gifts of the gods were visited upon them, not fitfully or capriciously, but seasonably both for the ploughing of the land and for the ingathering of its fruits.[35]

Greek religion was focused on immediate or medium-term results, not eternal salvation[36] and, as such, it was of a votive nature, i.e., "giving something pleasing to the gods, including prayers, libations, and sacrifices, [which] was to establish a reciprocal relationship of trust with them that might lead to their favor."[37] As Theophrastus[38] put it, "One must sacrifice to the gods for three purposes: to give honor, to show gratitude, or because of one's need for good things."[39] With a world possibly full of an infinite number of gods there was always another to ask if their first choice did not produce what was asked. Through the making of vows, their fulfillment, and then paying these out, there was an interdependence between men and gods to achieve each other's aims.[40] The gods were not obliged to act, neither were the worshipers obligated to accept silence. They could ask again or simply

---

35. Isocrates, *Arop.* 7.30. This was a long-lived belief. Isocrates lived 436–338 BC and the same belief in *eusebia* is found in Aelius Aristides (AD 117–81). Aristides, *Or.* 24.42.

36. Rogers, *Mysteries of Artemis*, 15, 21.

37. Rogers, *Mysteries of Artemis*, 16.

38. Theophrastus (ca. 371–287 BC) studied under Plato and was the successor to Aristotle.

39. Rogers, *Mysteries of Artemis*, 16.

40. Rogers, *Mysteries of Artemis*, 19.

move on to a different god and keep trying until an answer was received. With religion based on results it was experimental and adaptive.[41] It needed to be adaptive as their world was precarious with the continual threat of everything from wars, famine, earthquakes through to plagues. At the heart of this belief system was an acceptance that the gods did not love all people equally. Individual trials and tribulations that may pose problems for Christians simply reinforced the worldview of polytheists.[42]

The worship of Artemis Ephesia lasted a long time and her image, which changed over time, was the main symbol, not just of the goddess, but also of the city and its people. The original image is thought to have started with a simple *xoanon*[43] which was adorned with clothes and jewelry.[44] A new statue was carved[45] in the sixth century BC presumably for Croesus's new temple. This image did not have the multiple "breasts" of later images.[46] It is unlikely this image survived the fire that destroyed Croesus's temple.[47] Coins from the third century BC[48] show the traditional huntress but, from the second century BC, she is shown in the form we now know as Artemis Ephesia[49] which

41. Rogers, *Mysteries of Artemis*, 31.
42. Rogers, *Mysteries of Artemis*, 276.
43. A simple carved image in which the original stone or wood is easily seen. Many of Artemis's statues are made of two materials with a dark head and hands suggesting a dark wooden statue under the cloths. LiDonnici, "Image of Artemis," 391. The gold and ivory figurines deposited in the foundations of the temple show such a statue. LiDonnici, "Image of Artemis," 404.
44. LiDonnici, "Image of Artemis," 391.
45. Remembered as being carved by Endoios who worked in Athens in the middle of the sixth century BC.
46. Strabo reports that the image at Marseilles was a copy of the sixth-century image and the copies from France do not show the multiple breasts. Strabo, *Geogr.* 4.1.4.
47. LiDonnici, "Image of Artemis," 400.
48. Ephesus was one of the great mints of Asia Minor. See an illustrated history and mythology of Ephesus in coins on the Macquarie University website: https://web.archive.org/web/20080219231747/http://learn.mq.edu.au/webct/RelativeResourceManager/15043963001/Public%20Files/index.htm.
49. Thomas, "At Home," 92. The earliest representation is on a coin from

4. EPHESIAN ARTEMIS

shows ornamentation that is common to deities throughout the cities of Hellenistic and Roman Anatolia.

Many copies and reproductions of the cult image of Ephesian Artemis remain. Her many "breasts"[50] have been said to reflect her ability to nurture[51] rather than her virginity which is associated with Greek Artemis. Her body and legs are enclosed in a tapering pillar[52] from which her feet protrude. This is a feature more associated with Near-Eastern and Egyptian deities, rather than Greek. Her later image had bands of animals on her torso and also by her side in keeping with her role as the "Mistress of Beasts"[53] in the sense that she was in command of all the wild animals. Paradoxically, she protects the young of wild animals while she herself is a hunter and the goddess of hunters.[54] Artemis was so aggressive that she mocked her brother Apollo for his cowardice.[55] It is quite possible that Paul's reference to fighting wild beasts (1 Cor 15:32) could be referring metaphorically to the forceful and dangerous opposition to the gospel by the followers of Artemis.[56]

---

ca. 133 BC. She is presented this way in the Salutaris inscription from AD 104. Trebilco, *Early Christians*, 23.

50. The protrusions from her upper body have been interpreted as a variety of objects. Three statues have nipples, but similar "breasts" appear on a male god, Zeus Labraundos from Anatolia. Whatever their origin, they may well have been viewed as breasts from the later imperial period. Thomas, "At Home," 86–87. They were certainly understood that way by third- and fourth-century Christian writers. LiDonnici, "Image of Artemis," 392. Given that the bee was a symbol of Artemis, another alternative is that they originally represented the hives of wild bees which were built next to each other and looks like breasts, "mastoeideis." Skarmintzo, "Cult of Artemis," 271. They may also represent the testicles of bulls sacrificed to her (they are about the right size). Knibbe, "Via Sacra," 142. Another suggestion is that they represent leather pouches filled with magic charms and fetishes.

51. LiDonnici, "Image of Artemis," 411.
52. Called a "term."
53. Homer, *Iliad*, 21.470.
54. Hjerrild, "Near Eastern Equivalents," 42.
55. Homer, *Iliad*, 21.470.
56. Hooker, "Artemis," 44.

The signs of the zodiac were displayed around her neck which proclaimed to the worshipers that she "possessed an authority and power superior to that of astrological fate."[57] The *Ephesia Grammata* (Ephesian letters) were written indistinctly and obscurely around the feet, girdle, and crown of Artemis indicating she has a direct connection with magic.[58] Pausanias the Lexicographer says that there were six "Ephesian Letters"[59] inscribed on the image of Ephesian Artemis.

Of the radical difference between the images of classical Greek Artemis and Artemis Ephesia it has been said:

> Artemis of Ephesos may or may not have many "breasts," a debatable point, but she certainly has two faces, or more properly, two bodies in both iconography and literature. One body is that of the traditional virgin goddess, the huntress of myth, as found in other Greek poleis. The other body, despite the sweet virginal face resembling that of her outdoor namesake, seems to belong to an ancient Anatolian goddess. In one form Artemis skirts over the mountains in a light tunic; in the other she stands rigidly imprisoned in a ponderously embroidered type of straitjacket, the "ependytes."[60] She seems to struggle to lift her arms, heavily weighed down by what the Fathers of the Church identified as breasts, and unable to take a step. Whatever the body language involved, both forms apparently belonged to the same person, at least in the late Hellenistic and Roman period.[61]

Coins minted at Ephesus sometimes show her with a mural crown (like a defensive city wall) which was similar to Cybele. (Cybele was a Phrygian goddess worshiped in Anatolia from Neolithic times and was considered by the Greeks to be a deification of the

---

57. Arnold, "Ephesus," 21.
58. Arnold, "Ephesus," 22–23.
59. McCown, "Ephesia Grammata," 129. Pausanias the Lexicographer is different from the geographer of the same name. Refer to the section "Magic" in Ephesus where the "Ephesian Letters" are explained.
60. An oriental prestige garment.
61. Brenk, "Artemis," 157.

4. EPHESIAN ARTEMIS

earth mother.) This suggests some merging of the two deities. Other coins show her with a torch symbolizing her nocturnal nature.[62] Acts 19:35 refers to an image that fell from heaven. Though there is no other known reference to this phenomenon in relation to Ephesus, the claim of heavenly origins of the image would have helped her claim for great transcendent power.[63] The goddess could be seen in other ways than through her image. There are many references to Artemis appearing in dreams[64] and also in epiphanies.[65]

What we know of the attitudes to this and other images in antiquity is usually in the context of debates among a small circle of highly educated elites or in the context of attacks on Christians or by Christians.[66] Even giving allegiance to a certain school of philosophy did not mean that a person would be consistent in their attitude to the images.[67] It is difficult to say how the average Ephesian worshiper understood her image, but it was a fundamental element of the cult. During the fourth to sixth centuries the cult became free of a central image and sacrifices but her worship continued.[68] Sometimes in Greek and Roman consciousness, the idols were treated as the god's themselves, or as a "faint reflection of their nature or active presence while at other times they approached them as the material products of human artifice."[69] It is likely that the worshipers came with many different understandings and at the very least they were "an acceptable and time-honoured means of honouring the divine."[70]

While Artemis Ephesia provided safety to the city and to those who fled to her sanctuary, there was a personal side to her

---

62. Knibbe, "Via Sacra," 153.
63. Arnold, *Ephesians*, 22.
64. Achilles Tatius, *Leuc. Clit.* 4.1.4; Strabo, *Geogr.* 4.1.3–4.
65. Strelan, *Paul, Artemis, and the Jews*, 52.
66. Deligiannakis, "Religious Viewing," 272, 186.
67. Deligiannakis, "Religious Viewing," 173, 175.
68. Deligiannakis, "Religious Viewing," 169–70.
69. Deligiannakis, "Religious Viewing," 172.
70. Deligiannakis, "Religious Viewing," 188.

worship as she was said to hear prayers and was savior and helper.[71] Artemis Ephesia was also a god who helped in times of transitions. Frequently Artemis is shown as standing in a doorway suggesting that she was the one who helped across thresholds.[72] She is sometimes called *Lysizones*, "the releaser of the girdle." Girls put this on at puberty and removed it after their first intercourse at which time it was dedicated to Artemis.[73] Up to this time they were like Artemis, virginal and not needing a male partner. The transition from maiden to married life may have involved the maiden fleeing (like the Amazons) from her father's house to Artemis's statue only to be wrenched away by the male.[74]

As already mentioned, according to the myths, Leto, a Titan,[75] was impregnated by Zeus and conceived twins—the daughter was Artemis and the son, Apollo. The myth continues that, at that time, when Leto was giving birth at the Ortygia, young men, called *kouretes*, frightened Hera out of her wits by making a deafening din by clashing their spears against their shields and shouting.[76] Artemis was born first and became the midwife for the delivery of her brother. This act saw her as being the god who protected in childbirth.[77] Her temple was destroyed, it was claimed, by an arsonist in 356 BC.[78] However, this was given a positive "spin" by presenting this an example of Artemis's help through childbirth, as this calamity occurred on the same night that Alexander the Great was born. The excuse given by Plutarch for Artemis not looking after her temple was that she was too preoccupied with Alexander's

---

71. Strelan, *Paul, Artemis, and the Jews*, 51.
72. Strelan, *Paul, Artemis, and the Jews*, 51.
73. Strelan, *Paul, Artemis, and the Jews*, 49.
74. Strelan, *Paul, Artemis, and the Jews*, 50.
75. According to Hesiod (probably writing about 700 BC) there were ten Titans and were the children of Uranus (sky) and Gaia (earth). They in turn were the parents of the first generation of Olympian gods. Hesiod, *Theog.* 915–29.
76. Strabo, *Geogr.* 14.1.20.
77. Callimachus, *Hymn. Dian.* 20–25.
78. Strabo, *Geogr.* 14.1.22.

4. EPHESIAN ARTEMIS

delivery to save her burning temple.[79] The importance of her role as protectress cannot be underestimated. When Paul was in Ephesus, the girls were normally married in their early to mid-teens and very likely died in their mid-twenties and, if they lived, could be a grandmother in their thirties. Death during childbirth was so common that a successful delivery would be received with deep relief and viewed as an escape.[80] This god was also the protector of young men,[81] and men worshiped her in private.[82]

The relationship between Artemis Ephesia and her followers has been described as a "substance" relationship. Her power, which she was willing to dispense to her followers, flowed something like electricity. Herodotus gives an example of the city being protected from attack by Croesus by a rope running from the temple to the city.[83] This is different from the prophetic-salvation-historical line of the Old Testament where God accomplished his own will through those who exercised faith.[84]

Much more is known about Artemis's temple than her rituals and festivals. However, her worship was known to involve the sacrifice of various animals and offering incense and so is not believed to be very different from that of other pagan deities. On some days a number of bulls would be offered in a bloody sacrifice.[85] The best-known festivals were the *Ephesia* held in the month of *Artemision* (late March/early April), the *Thargelion* (May/June) and the *Artemisia* (date uncertain)[86] It was impious and illegal to transact business on certain holy days and Artemis

---

79. Plutarch, *Alex.* 3.3–5.
80. Baugh, "Foreign World," 42, 53.
81. Strabo, *Geogr.* 14.1.20.
82. Strelan, *Paul, Artemis, and the Jews*, 53.
83. Herodotus, *Hist.* 1.26.
84. Arnold, *Ephesians*, 36.
85. Knibbe, "Via Sacra," 142.

86. References to these festivals are only found from imperial times but there are inscriptions from after the middle of the second century that record that the *Epheseia* had been performed over 500 times. Van der Linde, "Artemis Ephesia," 181.

is reported to have killed her followers for neglecting her ceremonies.[87] Xenophon of Ephesus's account of the festival of *Artemisia* in his novel, *Ephesiaka* presents it as a time for young men and women to find their fiancés.[88] *Thargelion*, which celebrates the birthday of Artemis, is discussed under the *Mysteries of Artemis*. *Ephesia and Artemisia* are known to have featured all types of contests and music was emphasized along with dance. Aelian described one of these during the Ephesia:

> The sweet maidens, daughters of Lydia, sport and lightly leap and clap their hands in the temple of Artemis, the Fair at Ephesus, now sinking down on their haunches and again springing up like the hopping wagtail.[89]

An unusual feature of her worship was processions. One of the three annual processions was a circuit of Panayir Dagh which was originally a circular cemetery right around the mountain.[90] At least 260 people were involved with a procession of thirty-one gold and silver type statues from the temple through the city and back again to mark days the assembly met, important festivals and other events. This was probably as frequently as every two weeks and would have impacted traffic in the city.[91] This all made for an opportunity for the whole community to be unified through involvement in public and explicit participation of her worship. A second-century AD inscription refers to the improvements in the way these festivals and sacrifices honored Artemis which ensured, "our city will remain more illustrious and more blessed for all time."[92]

She was served by eunuchs and virgins though, by Strabo's time, the use of eunuchs, in effect male equivalents of the virgins,

---

87. Oster, "Ephesian Artemis," 38.

88. Xenophon, *Ephesiaka*, 1.2.2–4

89. Aelian, *Nat. an.* 12.9.

90. Knibbe, "Via Sacra," 142.

91. Trebilco, *Early Christians*, 28. The details are known from a very large inscription on the theatre wall known as the Salutaris Inscription.

92. Trebilco, *Early Christians*, 27.

4. EPHESIAN ARTEMIS

had ceased.[93] Pausanias, 200 years later, would say that Artemis was served by priests, called king bees, who would be chaste for twelve months, not eunuchs.[94] There has been reference found to both a high priest and priestess.[95] The presence of priests was unusual for a Greek city as goddesses were normally served by priestesses and the gods were served by priests.[96] By the start of the second century the chief official at the temple was a priestess.[97]

Artemis was presented as a personal savior and helper[98] who heard prayers. *Ephesiaka*,[99] a novel about two young lovers by Xenophon, has a plot far more twisted and improbable than any soap opera. It shows how Artemis is able to preserve, through many trials, two lovers who want to remain faithful to their vows.[100] Artemis "is seen as a champion of chastity, not in a ritual context but in everyday behavior, that is, a supporter of chastity as a moral value, a conventional Greek attitude."[101] A detailed word picture is painted in this novel of the goddess during a procession which is of the classic virgin huntress.[102]

When Lysimachus built the new city of Arsinoeia naming it after his Egyptian wife, it was not just an improved and healthier Ephesus but also an attempt to build his own city outside the interference of Artemis and her priests.[103] This was not completely successful and the name, at least, quickly reverted to Ephesus

93. Strabo, *Geogr.* 14.1.23.

94. Pausanias, *Descr.* 8.13.1.

95. Baugh, "Among the Amazons," 167.

96. Baugh, "Foreign World," 35.

97. Trebilco, *Early Christians*, 21.

98. Strelan, *Paul, Artemis and the Jews*, 51. Pausanias makes numerous references to Artemis being called "savior" throughout the Greek world, e.g., 1.40.2; 1.44.4; 3.22.12; 3.23.10.

99. Two of the five preserved Greek novels are centered on Ephesus which give us a good look into religion and life in Ephesus.

100. This same concept can be seen in the attempted rape in Achilles Tatius's *Leucippe and Clitophon*. Achilles Tatius, *Leuc. Clit.* 6.21.2.

101. Thomas, "At Home," 96.

102. Xenophon, *Eph.* 1.2.6–7.

103. Knibbe, "Via Sacra," 144.

53

after Lysimachus's death. But it was no longer just the priests and priestesses "who mediated relations with the goddess or even defined her through the performance of rituals."[104] Later Augustus tried to address the same problem of the power of the Artemision through giving Artemis back all the rights and property taken during the civil war, with the hope she would give up her claim to the city.[105] While access to the temple could be difficult, the worship of Artemis inside the city was already established with her image installed inside and outside the prytaneion, the seat of government, where she ruled with Hestia Boulaia. The latter may have served as her ambassador.[106]

Strabo also said that on her birthday, sixth of Thargelion (late April/early May), that mysteries were performed but does not elaborate.[107] Little is known of the spiritual significance and nature of these mysteries, but they are explored in the section *Mysteries of Artemis*. After the changes made by Lysimachus a second sanctuary at Ortygia was given increased importance. The mysteries by which Artemis could be worshiped in a different way would be outside of the control of the temple and its functionaries. Inscriptions have been found that indicate that mystery rites were practiced, and the celebration of her birth was one of the major occasions for the performance of these mysteries.[108] Magic and mysteries could be linked and as mentioned, the worship of Artemis was also associated with the practice of magic. The city "gained somewhat of a reputation as being a center for magical practices in Antiquity."[109]

The reciting of myths which explained the relationship of Ephesus to its gods and heroes was an important part of her worship. Some of these were secret and were related to a specific festival and time.[110] They could be used to initiate into the tribe, bring

---

104. Rogers, *Mysteries of Artemis*, 85–86.
105. Knibbe, "Via Sacra," 146.
106. Knibbe, "Via Sacra," 146.
107. Strabo, *Geogr.* 14.1.20.
108. Arnold, "Ephesus," 250.
109. Arnold, "Ephesus," 250.
110. Strabo, *Geogr.* 14.1.20,

4. EPHESIAN ARTEMIS

salvation, and give meaning through continuity with the past.[111] By remembering her myths, the reciter was calling upon the creative and sustaining power of Artemis. When the Greeks had to justify to Rome the retention of temple asylum, the Ephesians did so by reciting their myths.[112] The myths are said to be "maps" which "expressed the life-power of Ephesus."[113] It is possible that only Ionians (those descended from Ion of Athens) owned and controlled these myths[114]

Initially gods were seen as local deities but during the Hellenistic period some, such as Artemis and Isis were no longer understood as limited in their sphere of influence to their locality but were raised to become universal. Despite rising to a celestial realm, Artemis Ephesia still retained her strong connection to the city.[115] During the Roman period, Greek Artemis was seen as a unity with Diana and Isis and likewise Ephesian Artemis was also associated with these two, particularly Isis who had a very political role in Egypt as Artemis Ephesia did in Ephesus.[116] This close linking to Isis in her form as nursing Isis may have suggested a way of enhancing their understanding of attributes already implied in Artemis Ephesia.

The famous statement by Demosthenes about the roles of women in Greek culture, "Mistresses we keep for the sake of pleasure, concubines for the daily care of our persons, but wives to bear us legitimate children and to be faithful guardians of our households,"[117] has bearing on understanding the role of Artemis Ephesia. Western culture tends to eroticize all female roles but not so the Greek. The goddess is fully gendered, but she is not sexual.

---

111. Strelan, *Paul, Artemis and the Jews*, 55.
112. Tacitus, *Ann.* 3.61.1.
113. Strelan, *Paul, Artemis and the Jews*, 57.
114. Strelan, *Paul, Artemis and the Jews*, 68.
115. Martin, *Hellenistic Religions*, 58–9.
116. LiDonnici, "Image of Artemis," 407.
117. Demosthenes, [*Neaer.*] 59.122. Herodotus is surprised and suspicious about the concept of a man being sexually obsessed with his wife. Herodotus, *Hist.* 1.8–12.

Hanging breasts were seen as grotesque in erotic art whereas in a wife and mother they were to be respected. In her "nutrient breasts that overflow with sustaining milk"[118] she would be seen rather as the legitimate wife of the city and protectress of family, providing political and even the universe's stability. Therefore, Artemis could be worshiped by virgins, celibate priestesses, and married women without any paradox.[119] Her female devotees took pride in their modest piety.[120]

The edicts of Theodosius in AD 381 forbade the worship of pagan gods but the worship of Artemis was already in decline.[121] The second century saw the educated turning to philosophy while the uneducated turned to Christianity or one of the myriad of new religions, particularly oriental.[122] These were seen as providing better "answers to human concerns, especially to the crucial question of life after death."[123] As access to Artemis's temple was always difficult in the wet and with changed perspectives and expectations, fewer people were prepared to put up with this difficulty so they simply stayed at home.[124]

Artemis prospered during the period AD 50–150 even increasing in strength and "was well known throughout the world for her goodness and for the success she had bought to Ephesus."[125] In the third century, Artemis remained strong with her image still on Ephesian coins.[126] The second-century AD novel of Achilles Tatius shows her as the only one who can save. As Artemis fought

---

118. LiDonnici, "Image of Artemis," 408.

119. LiDonnici, "Image of Artemis," 410. Graves's statement that, in Ephesus, Artemis was worshiped in a second form "as nymph, an orgiastic Aphrodite with male consort" seems contradictory to this view. Graves, *Greek Myths*, 87.

120. Baugh, "Among the Amazons," 163.

121. Knibbe, "Via Sacra," 146.

122. Knibbe, "Via Sacra," 146.

123. Knibbe, "Via Sacra," 148–9.

124. Scherrer, "City of Ephesos," 9.

125. Strelan, *Paul, Artemis and the Jews*, 80.

126. Strelan, *Paul, Artemis and the Jews*, 81.

4. EPHESIAN ARTEMIS

for her survival, she was given roles that she did not exercise earlier, such as Asclepius,[127] to make her appear more helpful. Statues dating from the Roman period show her with a Zodiac neck ornament which suggests a conceptual change of associating her with the impersonal forces of astrology.[128]

Artemis withstood Christianity till the fourth century and was still seen as a rival to it.[129] The fallen statues of Artemis slightly damaged during the earthquakes ca. AD 400 were buried by the Christians.[130] Christians were claiming victory by early in the fifth century[131] and in AD 435 the Roman emperors signed an edict condoning the destruction of the images.[132] But victory was not as clear cut as the public destruction of images as grave artefacts show that Pagan activity continued into the fifth century.[133] Three centuries after Constantine, paganism was still strong as John of Ephesus (ca. AD 507–88) claimed to have converted 80,000 pagans and overcome the idols.[134] Even as late as the eighth century there were problems of Christians lapsing into paganism.[135]

The Temple of Artemis

In ancient Greece, the sanctuaries of Artemis were often located in a mountainous region and close to rivers and marshes which would water the grove of trees that was associated with her temples. This was the case for the Artemision, the name given to the temple at Ephesus and the Ortygia, some distance away[136] where her mysteries were celebrated. Only superlatives have been used to

127. The demigod of healing and medicine.
128. LiDonnici, "Image of Artemis," 407.
129. Strelan, *Paul, Artemis and the Jews*, 81.
130. Scherrer, "City of Ephesos," 19.
131. Strelan, *Paul, Artemis and the Jews*, 81.
132. Rogers, *Mysteries of Artemis*, 284.
133. Knibbe, "Via Sacra," 151.
134. Trombley, "Paganism in the Greek World," 330–31.
135. Trombley, "Paganism in the Greek World," 347.
136. Rogers, *Mysteries of Artemis*, 37.

describe the Artemision which became synonymous with Ephesus itself. Antipater of Sidon (second century BC) who compiled the famous seven wonders of the ancient world said of the temple of Artemis, "I have set eyes on the wall of lofty Babylon on which is a road for chariots, and the statue of Zeus by the Alpheus, and the hanging gardens, and the colossus of the Sun, and the huge labor of the high pyramids, and the vast tomb of Mausolus; but when I saw the house of Artemis that mounted to the clouds, those other marvels lost their brilliancy, and I said, 'Lo, apart from Olympus, the Sun never looked on aught (anything) so grand."[137]

Remains of the temple of Artemis with a recreated pillar

Croesus promoted the worship of the "goddess of Ayasoluk" (the hill near where the Artemision would be built) into the Greek Artemis. This was a political decision and long predates Lysimachus's decision to decide who the savior was and how she was to be worshiped. Pausanias refers to Croesus's temple being built over an existing structure,[138] and his large marble temple was built over two competing cultic centers at the one site. It is

137. Antipater of Sidon, *Anth. Pal.* 9.58.
138. Pausanias, *Descr.* 7.2.7; Callimachus, *Hymn. Dian.* 237–40, 248–50.

4. EPHESIAN ARTEMIS

said, "Kroisos intended to unify this important region of his kingdom under the religious government of one mighty goddess."[139] Even Croesus's temple was claimed to be four times the size of the temple at Athens. It is possible that Croesus "might have seen the Artemision as a Greek architectural expression of devotion to the Anatolian goddess, the patroness worshiped in Asia Minor from time immemorial."[140]

Archaeologists have identified three previous structures prior to that of Croesus, which are called temples A to C.[141] The foundations for the first large temple (temple D) were commenced ca. 600 BC and Herodotus said the columns were erected by ca. 560 BC.[142] Croesus paid for these columns and fragments have been found which say, "donated by King Croesus."[143] Construction continued under different architects until its completion about 220 years afterwards. While the story of the destruction of the temple by arson in 356 BC[144] on the same night that Alexander the Great was born was convenient,[145] geological changes may have been more to blame. It is possible that Croesus's temple was sinking into the swamp and a new temple needed to be built.

Pliny the Elder (AD 23–79) described[146] the construction of the final temple and said that it:

> took one hundred and twenty years in building, a work in which all Asia joined. A marshy soil was selected for its site, in order that it might not suffer from earthquakes, or the chasms which they produce. On the other hand, again, that the foundations of so vast a pile might not have to rest upon a loose and shifting bed, layers of trodden charcoal were placed beneath, with fleeces covered

139. Knibbe, "Via Sacra," 143.
140. Brenk, "Artemis," 165.
141. Oster, "Ephesus," 545.
142. Herodotus, *Hist.* 1.92.
143. Oster, "Ephesus," 544.
144. Strabo, *Geogr.* 14.1.22.
145. Plutarch, *Alex.* 3.3–5.
146. Pliny the Elder, *Nat.* 36.21.14.

with wool upon the top of them. The entire length of the temple is four hundred and twenty-five feet (about 130 meters), and the breadth two hundred and twenty-five (about 69 meters). The columns are one hundred and twenty-seven in number, and sixty feet (about 18 meters) in height, each of them presented by a different king. Thirty-six of these columns are carved, and one of them by the hand of Scopas. Chersiphron was the architect who presided over the work.

He goes on to describe how the large stones were placed. The lintel was so large that, allegedly, it could only be placed with the assistance of the goddess herself.[147] It is estimated that each column supported in excess of 100 tons of marble.[148] The building was not completely covered as the walls enclosed an open court area called a *sekos*.

The temple was being rebuilt (Temple E, the building from Paul's time) during Alexander's conquest and the Macedonian offered to pay for the rebuilding providing he was given what we might understand as "naming rights." This was declined by the citizens of Ephesus who said that it was "inappropriate for a god to dedicate offerings to a god."[149] Foreign political domination carried with it the stigma of religious domination as religious artefacts had been appropriated to Sardis and Persian priests "had to be accommodated diplomatically within the worship of Artemis Ephesia."[150] By paying for the temple themselves the Ephesians may have been re-establishing the identity of the city, but they may well have been hedging their bets, as Alexander's victory was by no means certain.

147. Pliny the Elder, *Nat.* 36.21.95.
148. Muss, "Temple," 32.
149. Strabo, *Geogr.* 14.1.24.
150. LiDonnici, "Image of Artemis," 401.

4. EPHESIAN ARTEMIS

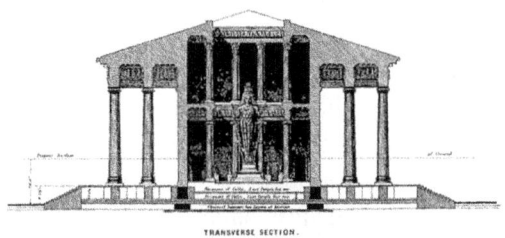

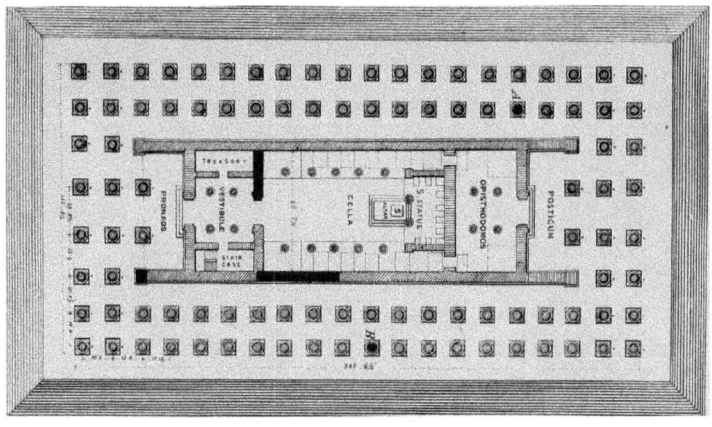

Wood's reconstruction of the temple of Artemis

The new temple was probably built on the same foundations as those of Croesus's and on a similar plan to the earlier temple but was far more magnificent using white marble stones that were up to 9.5 meters long. Even the roof tiles were marble.[151] The white marble was discovered thirteen kilometers away by a shepherd called Pixodarus[152] who, because of his discovery, was worshiped regularly under the auspices of the city's magistrates who would be legally punished if they did not comply.[153]

151. Muss, "Temple," 32.
152. Vitruvius, *De Arch.* 10.2.15.
153. Oster, "Ephesus," 545.

The temple was holy because it contained Artemis's image and the image remained central to the identity of Ephesus up to the third century.[154] Everyone could enter Artemis's temple except for married women who were excluded on penalty of death.[155] In the grove associated with the temple there was also a cave which contained pan pipes. A woman could prove whether she was a virgin or not by the sound given out by the pipes.[156] The temple itself also retold the myths of Ephesus through sculpture and paintings. There were at least four statues of the Amazons in the temple.[157] The walls recorded a multitude of civic inscriptions displaying decisions and awards and grants of citizenship.[158]

154. Strelan, *Paul, Artemis and the Jews*, 72.
155. Achilles Tatius, *Leuc. Clit.* 7.13.3.
156. Achilles Tatius, *Leuc. Clit.* 8.6.12.
157. Pliny the Elder, *Nat.* 34.19.53. Vitruvius, *De Arch.* 10.2.15.
158. Oster, "Ephesian Artemis," 34; Trebilco, *Early Christians*, 27.

4. EPHESIAN ARTEMIS

Column base from the British Museum

Most ceremonies took place at night[159] and frequently there were meals in the temple which had the implication of eating with the gods. Strangers were welcome and this bonded them to the citizens of Ephesus.[160] Citizenship was also granted by the priests at the temple.[161] There were obviously major social and theological implications for Jewish and Christian participation

159. Oster, "Ephesian Artemis," 33; Strelan, *Paul, Artemis and the Jews*, 71.
160. Strelan, *Paul, Artemis and the Jews*, 75.
161. Strelan, *Paul, Artemis and the Jews*, 75.

in these meals and ceremonies. Eating food sacrificed to idols was one of the four things forbidden to Christians by the Council of Jerusalem (Acts 15:29; 21:25).

Key to Greek religion was the belief that everything inside the sacred territory associated with a temple was owned by the respective god and what was owned by the gods was forbidden to men. This made precincts inviolable and along with that the often valuable offerings made to the gods. In Ephesus particularly, it made the temple the ideal location for a bank.[162] There were secular banks in the city, but the temple of Artemis was completely joined to Asia's economic world as it was "the common bank of Asia" and the "refuge of necessity."[163] With financial dependence came an entwining of the cultural life of Asia. Despite being pillaged in the fourth century BC and destroyed by fire; the imagination of the Roman writers was captured by the inviolability of the sanctuary.[164] Dio Chrysostom (ca. AD 40–120) describes the financial services offered by the temple:

> You know the Ephesians, of course, and that large sums of money are in their hands, some of it belonging to private citizens and deposited in the temple of Artemis, not alone money of the Ephesians but also of aliens and of persons from all parts of the world, and in some cases of commonwealths and kings, money which all deposit there in order that it might be safe, since no one has ever yet dared to violate that place. Although countless wars have occurred in the past and the city has often been captured.... They [the Ephesians] would sooner, I imagine strip off the adornments of the goddess than touch this money.[165]

About 400 money keepers were employed who loaned money on interest and took mortgages and ensured that payments were

---

162. Sinn, "Greek Sanctuaries," 72.
163. Aristides, *Pax.* 24.
164. Thomas, "At Home," 98.
165. Dio Chrysostom, *Or.* 31.54-55.

4. EPHESIAN ARTEMIS

made.[166] Artemis also controlled large estates with vineyards, along with quarries, pastures and salt pans,[167] collected fishing tolls[168] and also had sacred deer.[169] A very large income was needed as the Artemisium also had to care for several smaller temples located in other cities as well as the suburbs of Ephesus.[170] With so much money involved it would be expected that there would have been considerable decadence. Philostratus described the decadence of this place by quoting Apollonius of Tyana, a charismatic teacher and miracle worker from the first century AD who allegedly said:

> The first discourse then which he delivered was to the Ephesians from the platform of their temple, and its tone was not that of the Socratic school; for he dissuaded and discouraged them from other pursuits, and urged them to fill Ephesus with real study rather than with idleness and revelry such as he found around him there; for they were devoted to dancers and taken up with pantomimes, and the whole city was full of pipers, and full of effeminate rascals, and full of noise. So, though the Ephesians had come over to him, he determined not to wink at such things, but cleared them out and made them odious to most of them.[171]

This corruption is not surprising considering how office bearers could be installed in the religious office at the Artemisium and in public office. As was normal in Hellenist cities, civil magistrates exercised control of the temple and Roman governors meddled in their affairs.[172] An inscription from AD 44 from the provincial proconsul Paullus Fabius Persicus includes:

> While using the appearance of the divine temple as a pretext, they sell the priesthoods as if at public auction.

166. Strelan, *Paul, Artemis and the Jews*, 76.
167. Strelan, *Paul, Artemis and the Jews*, 76.
168. Strabo, *Geogr.* 14.1.26.
169. Strabo, *Geogr.* 14.1.29.
170. Oster, "Ephesian Artemis," 36.
171. Philostratus, *Vit. Apoll.* 4.2.
172. Baugh, "Foreign World," 37–38.

Indeed, they invite men of every kind to their sale, then they do not select the most suitable men upon whose head the crown would fittingly be placed.[173]

Around the temple, an area[174] of refuge was set aside as a haven for criminals. This area was also a refuge for men fleeing creditors, and politicians who found their lives threatened[175] and even for slaves from their masters.[176] The area around the temple had been an area of refuge prior to the construction of Temple E, and the practice continued. This right is said to originate in mythological times when the Amazons sought refuge there when they were defeated first by Dionysus[177] and then Herakles.[178] The area of refuge continued to grow but when the area allowed for refuge was too great "it proved harmful and put the city in the power of criminals."[179] Augustus restored the boundaries for asylum back to its original area. Further, he separated any legal connection between the temple and the city and at least sanctioned the removal of the *Kouretes* (who administered the mysteries of Artemis) from the temple to the secular administrative center, the *prytaneion*.[180] This is more radical than anything Lysimachus had done almost three centuries earlier. The standards for asylum had become lax, and not just in Ephesus. Tiberius revoked the asylum rights of many temples and probably caused Ephesus to be more responsible with theirs. This sanctuary led the temple to be characterized as the "last

---

173. Baugh, "Foreign World," 37–38.

174. Strabo reports these changes. Strabo, *Geogr.* 14.1.23. The most famous distance was set when Mithridates shot an arrow from the corner of the temple roof. If the prison epistles were written from Ephesus, it is possible that the runaway slave Onesimus came to that city seeking safety, rather than Rome.

175. Thomas, "At Home," 100.

176. Strelan, *Paul, Artemis, and the Jews*, 70.

177. Also known as Bacchus. This son of Zeus was viewed as the promoter of civilization, a lawgiver, and lover of peace.

178. The son of Zeus and Alcmene who, by conquering dangerous archaic forces, was mankind's benefactor by making the world safe. Pausanias, *Descr.* 7.2.7.

179. Strabo, *Geogr.* 14.1.23; 11.14.1.

180. Rogers, *Mysteries of Artemis*, 167.

4. EPHESIAN ARTEMIS

hope of desperate Individuals, a haven of possible security of those battered by fate."[181] Stories of the sanctuary provided were legendary[182] but there were notable and grave abuses of this sanctuary including the slaughter of the Romans by the Ephesians during the Mithridatic wars[183] and of Cleopatra's siblings.[184]

As an indication of the intertwining of Artemis and the Imperial cult, inscriptions indicate that there was a *Sebasteion*, a cult place dedicated to Augustus located in the *temenos* (the land adjacent to a temple) of the Artemision from at least 6/5 BC and that it operated till the end of the second century.[185] A gymnasium was also known to have been built during the imperial period. Also mentioned are a hall with paintings[186] and a banqueting hall.[187]

The Artemision was situated well outside the later walled city but was connected to it by a sacred way. The temple was found by John Wood through following the remains of this path. It was built over what had been a shallow bay in Croesus's time but by the Hellenistic period the water had receded though the land remained boggy. Not until Roman times was the ground firm enough to build a permanent road[188] but the path frequently became impassable and people could not go to the temple even if they wanted to.[189] In an attempt to stop Artemis's decline in popularity a very costly covered marble walkway was built from the city to the temple, a

---

181. Thomas, "At Home," 103.

182. Aelian says that when Croesus marched on the city, ropes were strung from the city to the temple so adding the city to the temple sanctuary and so the city was saved. Aelian, *Var. hist.* 3:26.

183. Appian, *Mith.* 4.23.

184. Cassius Dio, *Hist. rom.* 48.24.2.

185. Van der Linde, "Artemis Ephesia," 174–5.

186. Pausanias, *Descr.* 10.38.6–7.

187. Philostratus, *Vit. Soph.* 2.23.2

188. Knibbe, "Via Sacra," 148.

189. Knibbe, "Via Sacra," 149.

distance of one stade (about 185 meters).[190] A second formerly covered walkway has now also been found.[191]

Temple E along with the city was badly damaged during the invasions of the Goths in AD 262 and was not rebuilt. Further destruction occurred in 401 when a mob, allegedly spurred on by John Chrysostom, the golden-mouthed preacher, stripped Artemis's image of its jewelry and then burnt it. A cross was placed where her image stood for hundreds of years. The temple was finally closed towards the beginning of the fifth century and because it was oriented with its main entrance facing the west, what was the open courtyard was re-consecrated as a church in the sixth century.[192] Subsequently, the stone would be quarried for building material for civic, Christian, and then Islamic buildings.[193]

The Mysteries of Artemis

Mysteries have been described as a secret initiation ritual of a voluntary and personal nature that "aimed at a change of mind through experience of the sacred."[194] Mysteries associated with the worship of Artemis were performed in the old classical city before the founding of Arsinoeia but, after the changes of Lysimachus, the emphasis was on mysteries conducted at a second site for the worship of Artemis. There her mysteries and sacrifices were performed in or near a grove of trees called Ortygia. (The site has not been definitely identified but the proposed locations put it about five hours walk either south or south-west of the center of Ephesus.)[195] At least forty-six inscriptions remain from the prytaneion, the center of civil administration from the time of Tiberius (AD 14–37) through to the end of the second century. They recount who

---

190. Philostratus, *Vit. soph.* 2.23.2.
191. Knibbe, "Via Sacra," 150.
192. Muss, "Artemision," 297, 309–10.
193. Muss, "Artemision," 310.
194. Rogers, *Mysteries of Artemis*, 16.
195. Rogers, *Mysteries of Artemis*, 8.

4. EPHESIAN ARTEMIS

administered the mysteries, what they wanted others to think of their contribution and, how they changed over time particularly in relation to the Roman administration.[196]

It was claimed that Leto had given birth to Artemis and Apollo under one of these trees.[197] The grove, named after Artemis's nurse, Ortygia contained smaller temples and statues. Some of these statues were very old and made from wood while in one of the later temples there was a family group carved by one of the best Greek sculptors, Skopas of Paros.[198] For roughly 500 years,[199] on the sixth of Thargelion (late April/early May) the Ephesians celebrated her birthday at Ortygia and the young men would again scare Hera away and be initiated and have Artemis's mysteries revealed to them. For the next year Artemis, who was saved by the Kouretes (young men), was expected to save them and the city of Ephesus. Something she did for hundreds of years.[200] At Ortygia, "the Ephesians connected and reconnected themselves each year to Artemis and to all the benefits she might bestow on them."[201]

Greek mysteries were initially thought to be a product of oriental influence and only introduced following the conquests of Alexander but it has since been shown now that they were practiced in the sixth century BC.[202] Mysteries were an alternative form of votive offering in a similar quest for immediate, not eternal salvation

---

196. Rogers, *Mysteries of Artemis*, 9–10.

197. Delos also claimed this honour. Callimachus, *Hymn Del.* 209–10. Early Ephesian coinage pictures a palm tree under which Leto is said to have given birth but Strabo says it was an olive tree. Strabo. *Geogr.* 14.1.20. Refer to the coin on page 7 from ca. 400 BC showing the stag and a palm tree.

198. Strabo, *Geogr.* 14.1.20. The mention of Skopas puts the dating of this sometime after 356 BC.

199. There are very extensive epigraphic records of two hundred years during the Roman period not only giving the names of the people involved but inferences can be drawn on what rituals were performed and how they changed over time. Rogers, *Mysteries of Artemis*, 10.

200. Rogers, *Mysteries of Artemis*, 3–4, 26.

201. Rogers, *Mysteries of Artemis*, 269.

202. Rogers, *Mysteries of Artemis*, 14. The earliest reference in Ephesus is from the fourth century BC.

after death.²⁰³ The initiation into these mysteries did not provide "salvation" in the Christian sense as the majority of Greco/Roman mystery cults are not seen as "helping ultimately against the certainty of death or what came after death."²⁰⁴ Still, people could pay large fees to be initiated into these religions.

In many Greek cities it was their councils and assemblies that had the legal, constitutional, and financial responsibility for the religious life of the city with its festivals and sacrifices.²⁰⁵ As such, political change would impact changes to the way religion was organized. The infrastructure of the city was needed for their fulfilment such as public baths for purification. For Lysimachus, a new structure of religious authority with no connection to the Artemision was probably as important as the infrastructure of the new city. Arsinoeia was distant from it and so freed, at least in part, from its theological authority.²⁰⁶ These changes would have been especially important in syncretizing a city that was being populated by the former citizens of Lebedos and Kolophon who had no connection to the Artemision.²⁰⁷ It is thought that Lysimachus, "wished to project his interpretation of Artemis as a Greek goddess of salvation outside the physical boundaries of the ancient, Persian dominated home of Artemis and the old classical polis of Ephesus."²⁰⁸

With the Ortygia situated close to the territory of cities that may not have been friendly, the presence of a sanctuary of a goddess who could save militarily was a powerful political message as well. A goddess that was a hunter had to be good with weapons. This new temple and statue of Artemis the savior with its mysteries along with the Gerousia sacrificing and feasting at the public expense may have helped integrate the new residents into one community. From inscriptions we know that the practice of the Gerousia feasting continued for a very long time.

    203. Rogers, *Mysteries of Artemis*, 16.
    204. Rogers, *Mysteries of Artemis*, 15.
    205. Rogers, *Mysteries of Artemis*, 25.
    206. Rogers, *Mysteries of Artemis*, 85.
    207. Rogers, *Mysteries of Artemis*, 85–86.
    208. Rogers, *Mysteries of Artemis*, 31.

4. EPHESIAN ARTEMIS

While participants in the mysteries where not shy in making this known, there are no known records of what the initiates[209] experienced as they entered Artemis's mysteries or what these secrets were[210] but in Apuleius's novel, *Metamorphoses*,[211] there is an account of Lucius's initiation into the mysteries of Isis in Cenchrea, the port of Corinth. After a very complicated story which involves deliverance from being transformed into an ass, the goddess appeared to Lucius and told him how much he had to spend on his initiation and that the high priest of Mithras was to perform the rites. He was then taken to Isis's temple and the priest read to Lucius from books with indecipherable writing which explained what preparations had to be made. He was taken to the public baths and cleansed. He was then taken to the temple and finally at the feet of the goddess was given secret instructions which were too holy to utter. After fasting for ten days, he was led to the inner part of the sanctuary and there:

> And now, diligent reader, you are no doubt keen to know what was said next, and what was done, . . . but I shall speak only of what can be revealed to the minds of the uninitiated without need for subsequent atonement, things which though you have heard them, you may well not understand. So listen, and believe in what is true. I reached the very gates of death and, treading Proserpine's[212] threshold, yet passed through all the elements

---

209. There is no definite reference to initiation of a secret nature occurring until the end of the first century but reference to mystic sacrifices and the participation of the *neoi* (a youth association) do point to initiation occurring from early times. Strabo, *Geogr.* 14.1.20.

210. Guy Rogers suggests that the "secret" revealed to the initiates, or better still experienced by them may have been "that the gods and mortals as a whole were dependent upon one another and that the Ephesians had played a key role in consolidating the Olympian dynasty." Rogers, *Mysteries of Artemis*, 277.

211. Dating from about AD 170, *Metamorphoses*, also known as *The Golden Ass*, is the only complete ancient Roman novel.

212. Proserpine (Greek) or Persephone (Latin) in Greek religion was the daughter of Zeus, the chief god, and Demeter, the goddess of agriculture. She was the wife of Hades, king of the underworld.

71

and returned. I have seen the sun at midnight shining brightly. I have entered the presence of the gods below and the presence of the gods above, and I have paid due reverence before them.[213]

Through continuous maintained tradition, mysteries could bring a sense of identity but, in Ephesus, kings, emperors, and governors rearranged, reorganized, and revitalized them for their own reasons.[214] The myth of the birth of Artemis at Ortega was central in the city's negotiations with Rome during the reign of Tiberius (AD 26) and their claims were apparently backed up by a written charter. Tacitus's account suggests that the story of Artemis birth at Ortygia was known right up to the emperor himself.[215] The mysteries became increasingly Romanized and secularized and new rituals added. The Kouretes, no longer young men but drawn from families of well-to-do Roman citizens, linked their reverence to Artemis with that of the emperor.[216] No longer was it only Artemis who was claimed to be the savior of Ephesus. The emperor was also now presented as savior to the city along with Artemis, as Ephesus had been of the Olympian gods, Artemis, and Apollo.[217]

By the middle of the second century the festival reached its greatest extent with more music, initiates, and sacrifices turning it into a tourist spectacle, but it reduced after the plague and possible famine of AD 166. Quite likely as a result of these disasters, the city and private benefactors reinvigorated the worship of Artemis and the emperor. In the third century large sections of the city were destroyed by an earthquake and the Artemision was plundered by the Goths in 262. Only then did the mysteries cease. The breakdown of the votive relation between mortals and immortals who lived in an interdependent community has been described as follows:

---

213. Apuleius, *Metamorphoses*, 11.23.
214. Rogers, *Mysteries of Artemis*, 31.
215. Tacitus, *Ann.* 3.60–63; 4.55–56.
216. Rogers, *Mysteries of Artemis*, 168, 170.
217. Rogers, *Mysteries of Artemis*, 278.

4. EPHESIAN ARTEMIS

Under renewed pressure during the third century AD, the polis and the individual benefactors in Ephesus tried various measures to re-establish the connection between themselves and their gods, only to find first that no one was at home and then that there was no home. It was only at this point that the Ephesians apparently stopped trying to mold their world through the celebrations of the great festival.[218]

The Kouretes were unable to gain a satisfactory response from Artemis, the emperor or any of the other gods they started to include in their mysteries and thanksgivings to the mounting problems facing Ephesus. This undermined confidence in and the social prestige of the city's rich saviors which could tear apart the interwoven fabric of religious and political authority. With that came into question the highly stratified and hierarchical order of Roman Ephesus.[219] That left the door open for new mediators of salvation. No longer would mortals and immortals be dependent on each other for salvation, and for many Ephesians, it was replaced with a religion that made better sense of the life they lived. At the heart of this religion would be another mother who gave birth to a saving God.

For all the mysteries long history and the numbers that were initiated it represented only a small portion of society, and these were the rich elite. It is not known if women were included in Artemis's mysteries. Christianity would welcome slaves and women and, as legend has it, their second bishop was a freed slave. At the top of society would come the poor loving bishops of Ephesus.

Cult Prostitution and Artemis

Cult prostitution can be defined:

> narrowly as union with a prostitute . . . for exchange of money or goods, which was sanctioned by the wardens of a deity whether in temple precincts or elsewhere as a

218. Rogers, *Mysteries of Artemis*, 273–74.
219. Rogers, *Mysteries of Artemis*, 281–82.

sacred act of worship. In such cases, the prostitute had semi-official status as a cult functionary, . . . and the sexual union is usually interpreted to have been part of a fertility ritual. More generally, cult prostitution could simply refer to acts of prostitution where the money or goods received went to a temple and to its administrators. In this latter case, the prostitutes would be slaves owned by the temple.[220]

Cult prostitution is well-known outside the Greek world in cities such as Comana in Pontus.[221] When describing the practice in that area, which is outside the main Greek sphere of influence, Strabo refers to the city as a little Corinth "On account of the multitude of harlots at Corinth, who are dedicated [possibly followers of] to Venus."[222] The practice of cult prostitution has always been assumed to have taken place at the Artemision based mainly on a reference to the practice in Corinth, another Greek city, which again we know from Strabo. Referring to classical times in Corinth,[223] he said:

> The temple of Venus at Corinth was so rich, that it had more than a thousand women consecrated to the service of the goddess, courtesans, whom both men and women had dedicated as offerings to the goddess. The city was frequented and enriched by the multitudes who resorted thither on account of these women. Masters of ships freely squandered all their money, and hence the proverb, "It is not in every man's power to go to Corinth."[224]

Strabo's reference was to the past and in his own time he would report that there was only a small temple of Venus in Corinth.[225]

---

220. Baugh, "Cult Prostitution," 444.

221. Strabo, *Geogr.* 12.3.36.

222. Strabo, *Geogr.* 12.3.36.

223. S. M. Baugh dates this to the reign of the tyrant Cypselus (657–25 BC). Baugh, "Cult Prostitution," 446.

224. Strabo, *Geogr.* 8.6.20.

225. Pausanias briefly describes this temple. Pausanias, *Descr.* 2.4.1. See also Strabo, *Geogr.* 8.6.21.

4. EPHESIAN ARTEMIS

Athenaeus[226] (ca. AD 200) also discusses the prominence of *hetairai*[227] in Corinth[228] but the context shows it as something extraordinary, particularly as participation in the state cults of any Greek city required a person to be a free citizen of that city.

Some now confidently assert that there was no cult prostitution in Ephesus."[229] Clearly the references to Corinth were to the goddess Aphrodite, not the Greek mother goddess, Demeter, nor was it to Artemis. One researcher confidently stated that neither:

> Strabo, Pliny the Elder, Dio Chrysostom, Pausanias, Xenophon of Ephesus, Achilles Tatius, nor any other ancient author speaks explicitly or even hints at cult prostitution in either the narrow or broad sense in Ephesus of any period. Nor is it evidenced in the nearly 4,000 extant Greek and Latin inscriptions from Ephesus.[230]

In Achilles Tatius's novel it is clear that Artemis's temple is not like that of Aphrodite as there is no sex there.[231] Prostitutes were absolutely excluded.[232]

By minimizing the importance of cult prostitution in Ephesus, this is not to say that Ephesus was not immoral. It was a large seaport and prostitution has always been associated with such places. But it seems to be just that, prostitution, not a participation in a fertility rite related to Artemis. (The presence or absence of cult prostitutes in Ephesus can have implications for

---

226. He is described as a "somewhat greasy heap of a literary rag-and-bone-picker" in the preface to the Loeb edition of his *Deipnosophistae* ("Table Talk"). Baugh says "it is clear that Athenaeus's knowledge of various customs is derivative and unfiltered gossip or literary snippets. He hardly serves as a stable historical source. Baugh, "Cult Prostitution," 448.

227. Hetairai were sophisticated companions and prostitutes. They were independent and frequently ex-slaves and foreigners. Unlike most women in Greek culture, they were often educated.

228. Athenaeus, *Deipn.* 13.573b–574c.

229. Baugh, "Cult Prostitution," 444; Oster, "Ephesus," 548.

230. Baugh, "Cult Prostitution," 444.

231. Achilles Tatius, *Leuc. Clit.* 5.21.4; 8.10.6.

232. Oster, "Ephesian Artemis," 28.

the interpretation of 1 Tim 2:9–15 and the discussion on the ordination of women.)[233]

---

233. E.g., Bobbie Hodgin asserts that "undoubtedly some of the new Christian converts had been cultic priestesses." Gritz, *Paul*, 116. This questions whether the "prominence of the sex-orientated mystery cult of Artemis would prompt a social, though non-Christian acceptability of sexual immorality." Gritz, *Paul*, 114. See also Payne: "The prominence of temple prostitutes in the Artemis worship of Ephesus would be an invitation to scandal if women in the church officiated in ways similar to those priestesses" Payne, "Libertarian Women," 183.

5. Other Pagan Religions

WHILE EPHESUS WAS THE cult center for the worship of Artemis Ephesia, there were also a number of traditional deities worshiped though they did not provide the long and sustained opposition and competition to Christianity that Artemis provided. This was no different from the situation in other large cities in the Greek east where there were many Greco-Roman and to a lesser extent, Anatolian deities as Table 1 illustrates.[1] Because Ephesus was at the interface between the east and the west, it "made it a veritable hotbed for the expansion of religions and cults."[2] While Rome had been described as the sewer of the Orontes[3] because of the impact of Syrian, Phrygian and Mithraic religions (frequently associated with very immoral practices), Ephesus remained Greek in its religion despite being an eastern city.[4] Christianity and Egyptian cults were the only ones to make a significant impact on the religious life of Ephesus.[5]

---

1. Oster, "Ephesus," 548. Add to this list Hestia who may have served as Artemis's ambassador in the city.
2. Oster, "Ephesian Artemis," 24.
3. Juvenal, *Sat.* 3.60–65.
4. Walters, "Egyptian Religions," 282.
5. Walters, "Egyptian Religions," 282.

77

Table 1. Pagan Religions in Ephesus[6]

Name	Literature	Coins	Epigraphy	Monuments
Aphrodite	*		*	
Apollo	*	*	*	*
Asclepius	*		*	
Athena	*	*	*	
Cabiri			*	
Demeter	*		*	*
Dionysus	*	*	*	*
Egyptian Cults	*	*	*	*
Ge			*	
God Most High			*	
Hecate	*	*	*	
Hephastus			*	
Hercules	*	*	*	*
Mother Goddess			*	*
Pluton			*	
Poseidon	*		*	
Zeus	*	*	*	*

Added to the pagan worship of Artemis and the traditional deities was the worship of select individuals, sometimes even while they were alive. This common practice among Greek cities has been described as the "pious and grateful response to unusual benefaction, to miraculous assistance, to extraordinary civic or

---

6. Oster, "Ephesus," 548.

5. OTHER PAGAN RELIGIONS

political contribution or to a unique role in the founding and history of the honoring city."[7]

Ephesian heroes include:

- Alexander the Great
- Androclus, the Greek founder
- Apollonius of Tyana for delivering the city from a plague
- Pixodarus Evangelos for discovering the marble from which the temple would be quarried, and
- Publius Servilius Isauricus, Roman proconsul 40–44 BC for his just treatment and advocacy of the city in official issues.[8]

Egyptian Cults

Egyptian religious artefacts have been found dating back to the seventh century BC,[9] but in the third century with the presence of Egyptian merchants and occupation by Egyptian forces, the worship of Egyptian gods became more prominent. Their worship is known to continue up to the fourth century AD.[10] It is possible that the widespread adoption of Egyptian deities in other cities during the reign of the Ptolemies, even when there was no occupation, may have been motivated by political considerations, not primarily religious ones.[11]

The cult gained prominence in the second century AD, the time of Christian expansion in Ephesus.

---

7. Oster, "Ephesus," 548.
8. Oster, "Ephesus," 548.
9. Walters, "Egyptian Religions," 282.
10. Walters, "Egyptian Religions," 304.
11. Walters, "Egyptian Religions," 286.

Imperial Cult

In a world of multiple gods, each with their own areas of responsibility, the emperor was a very important role as god of the Roman state, and so was important in maintaining the *pax deorum*, the god's peace.[12] If the gods were angry it resulted in civil wars, natural disasters, and disease. Augustus was the first emperor with the title *pontifex maximus* and through this role could restore and maintain the god's peace and along with that the peace and stability of the state.[13] The title given to the emperors, *divi*, represents the lowest rank of the gods, meaning the earthly rulers were not considered their equal but, through their wealth and power and status, were rather viewed as alongside the gods.[14]

The Ephesians must surely have seen the inconsistency in saying that Caesar, prone to illnesses and death, was god and in the fact that he would have sacrifices made to the other gods. Yet most of the evidence links the emperor with the gods.[15] This dichotomy of humanity and divinity was overcome by limiting the emperor's divinity to his spirit, not his body. Only his spirit ascended to the realm of the gods on his death.[16] Of course, "the worship of the emperor was an extension of diplomacy" and "was a way of representing power relationships."[17] In this way they did not honor the emperor so much as define him.[18]

The emperor, in a very visible way, was creating a world pleasing to the gods and so functioned like a god to the Ephesians.[19] The

---

12. Magyar, "Imperial Cult," 386.
13. Magyar, "Imperial Cult," 391.
14. Magyar, "Imperial Cult," 386.
15. An example is a letter to the Roman proconsul L. Mestrius Florus saying that mysteries and sacrifices "were made to Demeter Karpophoros and Thesmophoros, and to the gods Sebastoi by the initiates in Ephesus every year." Friesen, *Twice Neokoros*, 149.
16. Magyar, "Imperial Cult," 386, 391.
17. Friesen, "Roman Emperors," 242.
18. Friesen, "Roman Emperors," 242.
19. Friesen, *Twice Neokoros*, 150–53.

5. OTHER PAGAN RELIGIONS

gods in their turn protected the emperor[20] and the people could show their gratitude and dependence through the cult.[21] When Christians refused to sacrifice to the gods, they threatened the god's peace and along with it the stability of the state.[22]

There were practical reasons for supporting the worship of the emperor. To be a priest in the imperial religion was an important stepping stone for someone wanting a career in the provinces.[23] Another factor that advanced the imperial cult was that freed men barred from every other office were accepted into the college of the *severi Augustales* (priests of Augustus) and with the title came Roman citizenship. Wealthy freed slaves would give generously to the cult with a view to gaining membership to the order, to the extent that they were the main financial supporters.[24] His relationship with the normal person has been described as:

> Carr[ying] a new and positive sense of belonging to the Roman Empire. This Empire had a divine leader who, because of his divinity, was reachable through sacrifices. He was not a remote dictator anymore. If he was pleased, he poured his blessings on the community, if not, his curses. Hence, the imperial cult played a crucial role in the life of the local communities.[25]

We are likely to think of the worship of the god, Artemis, and the worship of the divine emperor, each with their own places of worship, priests, and rituals as two separate religions, each contending for the sole allegiance of the hearts of followers. But in Ephesus, empire-wide religious practices became completely intertwined not only with the local deity, but also the civic government as the city became increasingly Romanized. There are no inscriptions on buildings from the Roman period where the

---

20. Friesen, *Twice Neokoros*, 152.
21. Friesen, *Twice Neokoros*, 164.
22. Magyar, "Imperial Cult," 393.
23. Magyar, "Imperial Cult," 387.
24. Magyar, "Imperial Cult," 388–89.
25. Magyar, "Imperial Cult," 392.

dedication is solely to Artemis, but many are to the triad of Artemis, the emperor, and the city.

The interconnectivity between the imperial cult and Artemis can be seen in the use of *Neokoros*, the term that became synonymous with the Roman provincial cults and is Latin for temple warden. The term evolved from referring simply to a temple official through to its benefactor and finally to a city.[26] In Acts 19:35, Ephesus is also called the *neokoros* of Artemis. A coin from AD 65/66[27] refers to "Neokoros Ephesus" which probably means that the city was the *neokoros* of Artemis[28] though the term at this stage was unofficial. Later coins (ca. AD 211) would refer to Ephesus as being twice *neokoros* that of Artemis and the Sebastoi and then three times *neokoros*, showing that officially the cult of Artemis stood alongside and integrated with the imperial cult.[29] By this stage the imperial cult with its temples that dominated the skyline of the city had "infiltrated the fundamental essence and identity of Ephesos."[30]

During Augustus's time, the temples of Divus Julius and De Roma were built in Ephesus to serve the needs of provincial Romans which made little impact on local Ephesians at this stage. These municipal temples did not require the permission of the senate or emperor and became common[31] throughout Asia Minor.[32] At the instigation of the province,[33] approval was given in 29 BC to build a *neokoros* (though not termed that at the time) to Rome and Augustus in Pergamum for the use of Asians and foreigners.[34] Tacitus explains the rationale behind Rome's willing acceptance of

26. Friesen, "Roman Emperors," 229–30.

27. The only earlier reference to a city calling itself a *neokoros* is Kyzikos (in Mysia, Anatolia) in AD 38. Friesen, "Roman Emperors," 231.

28. Friesen, "Roman Emperors," 231.

29. Van der Linde, "Artemis Ephesia," 192.

30. Van der Linde, "Artemis Ephesia," 193.

31. At least thirty were established by AD 100. Gill, *Jesus as Mediator*, 51.

32. Gill, *Jesus as Mediator*, 51.

33. Cassius Dio, *Hist. rom.* 51.20.6.

34. Thomas, "At Home," 107.

5. OTHER PAGAN RELIGIONS

this request for a temple under Rome's control saying, "In the Greek cities license and impunity in establishing sanctuaries were on the increase. Temples were thronged with the vilest of the slaves; the same refuge screened the debtor against his creditor, as well as men suspected of capital offences. No authority was strong enough to check the turbulence of a people which protected the crimes of men as much as the worship of the gods"[35]

Augustus also introduced radical changes to the way Artemis was worshiped by firstly severing physical and legal ties between the Artemision with the city. The mysteries of Artemis at Ortygia, which after Lysimachus's reforms were administered by the city, not the Artemision, were being held to ritualize his triumph over Demetrios. They were in turn Romanized and implicated in Octavian's naval victory against Antony at Actium (off the west coast of Greece) in the civil wars. Octavian would then be granted the name *Augustus* by the Roman senate. This settled the question of who oversaw the celebration of Artemis's mysteries.[36] The Kouretes who organized the festival were formerly Greek priests or officials at the temple but instead became made up completely of Graeco-Roman elites.[37] This dual role in the secular and religious administration cemented their place in Ephesian culture. The history and identity of the city were tied up with the mysteries that were part of the celebration of the goddess' birth, and these gradually incorporated the godlike emperor. Not only Artemis but also the emperor was now presented as savior to the city of Ephesus, as the city had been of the Olympian gods when they protected the birth of Artemis, and Apollo.[38] We only have evidence of initiation taking place from the imperial time.

---

35. It is difficult to understand the validity of this argument as the traditional temples did not appear to lose their rights as sanctuaries. Tacitus, *Ann.* 3,60.

36. Rogers, *Mysteries of Artemis*, 267–68, 272.

37. Rogers, *Mysteries of Artemis*, 272. Kouretes means "youth" but following the reforms of 3–2 BC none were youths.

38. Rogers, *Mysteries of Artemis*, 278.

Approval was given in AD 26 for a second temple, this time to Tiberius, the then emperor, Livia (his mother and wife of Augustus) and the Senate to be built in Smyrna.[39] No province had been granted a second *neokoros* beforehand. Ephesus was rejected as the center because the worship of Artemis was too strong.[40] At the instigation of the "god" Gaius Caligula (AD 37–41, a living emperor) a third, short-lived *neokoros* not in association with anyone was in established in Miletus, again over Ephesus.[41]

Provincial temples were normally established for officially divinized emperors so to build a temple to a living Caesar was controversial.[42] Emperors in the later first century had no problems in following Gaius. On a high terrace that overlooked a Hellenistic residential area and the whole city, a temple of the *sebastoi* was built for Domitian[43] (emperor from AD 81–96) as *sebastos*[44] and possibly his wife Domita in Ephesus,[45] along with the other members of the Flavian family, Vespasian, and Titus.[46] This is a step different from from Gaius's position who deified an individual to then deifying a family. After Domitian's death and the *damnitio memoriae* whereby his memory was to be condemned, his name was removed but the cult was too firmly established. The plural *sebastoi* could still be associated with the other family members,[47] concentrating on Vespasian.[48] The temple prospered for another century.

39. Friesen, *Twice Neokoros*, 16.

40. Friesen, *Twice Neokoros*, 18.

41. Cassius Dio, *Hist. rom.* 59.28.1. Suetonius recounts his madness in the way he considered himself to be a god. Suetonius, *Cal.* 22.

42. Friesen, *Twice Neokoros*, 13,

43. Probably because of Domitian's opposition to corrupt Roman governors and starting to reform the tax system. Friesen, *Twice Neokoros*, 158, 160.

44. Literal Greek translation of the Latin term *Augustus*.

45. Friesen, *Twice Neokoros*, 36.

46. Friesen, *Twice Neokoros*, 48.

47. After Domitian's death there appeared to be no stigma associated with activities associated with Domitian or the strong provincial loyalty to the Flavians. Friesen, *Twice Neokoros*, 138.

48. Friesen, *Twice Neokoros*, 49.

5. OTHER PAGAN RELIGIONS

Neokoros is first known to be used officially on inscriptions on the bases of statues donated by the Asian cities in the temple of Flavian Sebastoi which was dedicated AD 88/91.[49] These inscriptions[50] show the tension between the cities and Ephesus over the establishment of the provincial imperial cult in Ephesus. "The free cities represented themselves as the ones who had bestowed the provincial temple on Ephesus, thereby placing Ephesus in their debt."[51] The Asian cities' attempt to have Ephesus view itself as simply a temple warden, the old meaning of the word, failed and the city would instead view itself as the benefactor.[52] The term *neokoros* would become a coveted title and appear at the beginning of public inscriptions from the beginning of the first century.[53]

Obverse: Septimius Severus (AD 193–211). Reverse: Septemius Severus and Caracalla, to either side of altar and cult statue of Ephesian Artemis

---

49. This timing may match the writing of Revelation as some see the establishment of the imperial cult as the reason for its writing. Friesen, *Twice Neokoros*, 44.

50. Thirteen of these have been found. Friesen, "Roman Emperors," 232.

51. Friesen, "Roman Emperors," 234.

52. Friesen, "Roman Emperors," 235.

53. Friesen, "Roman Emperors," 234. After Ephesus first used this title, many other cities would follow. Friesen, "Roman Emperors," 236–37.

During Domitian's reign, coins were issued referring to Ephesus as "twice *neokoros*" meaning that of Artemis and the Sebastoi.[54] It had two dominant and equal cults and all the citizens were the protectors of them.[55] This was a fundamental shift in how the city viewed itself, as now it was also tied to the worship of the emperor.[56] For Ephesus, the privilege would bring prominence in regional affairs, access to the best offices, religious tourists, entertainment, and new revenue streams.[57]

Market at the base of the imperial temple

54. Thomas, "At Home," 56.
55. Thomas, "At Home," 57.
56. Friesen, "Roman Emperors," 236.
57. Friesen, *Twice Neokoros*, 164.

5. OTHER PAGAN RELIGIONS

The images of the emperor followed a fairly standard format which never reflected him as aged, but "articulated different aspects of imperial rule, the civilian, military and divine [naked]."[58] By the time the Provincial cult was established in Ephesus there were known to be fifty statues to the emperor in the city.[59]

The city was transformed by the monumental civic construction associated with the imperial cult which served as areas for the celebration of the festivals associated with the worship of the emperor.[60] Buildings with a purely religious function were also built. A Greek-style temple (7.5 by 13 meters inside measurements and on a 34 by 24 meter base) was built on a large terrace (83.6 by 64.6 meters) on valuable land in the city center.[61] A redeveloped commercial area was also built adjacent to the temple with a colonnade of gods and goddesses, looked down upon by the temple which contained a very large statue of Titus.[62] This stated that the people's gods and goddesses supported the emperor and that the emperor, in his supreme role, united the religious systems of the people of the empire.[63]

The building of these large open spaces accommodated a unique feature of the Imperial cult. Religious ritual took place in the large open spaces built by the emperor outside of the confines of the traditional temples and sanctuaries.[64] Further, the common people were allowed to participate which actively helped to unify the city.[65] New festivals were established in the first, second, and third century along with a commemoration of the emperor's birthday and most continued well into the third century.

Athletic festivals were celebrated regularly during the imperial time and some games started to be associated with the cult,

58. Gill, *Jesus as Mediator*, 35–36.
59. Gill, *Jesus as Mediator*, 52.
60. Friesen, *Twice Neokoros*, 160.
61. Friesen, *Twice Neokoros*, 63–64, 66–67.
62. Friesen, *Twice Neokoros*, 60–61.
63. Friesen, *Twice Neokoros*, 75, 119.
64. Gill, *Jesus as Mediator*, 51.
65. Gill, *Jesus as Mediator*, 53.

EPHESUS: THE NURSERY OF CHRISTIANITY

the first being in Pergamum for Rome and Augustus.[66] At the same time the temple for the emperor was being built in Ephesus, the largest gymnasium and bath complex in Asia Minor were constructed. This complex combined a Roman bath, a palaestra,[67] and a traditional gymnasium, and so merged traditional Greek athletic values with Roman culture and hot water bathing.[68] The capital of Asia was a traditional Greek city but had developed Roman loyalties. These buildings, constructed near the harbor, measured 360 meters long by 240 meters wide and were built to host the Ephesian Olympics held in honor of Domitian.[69] In this way the complex became associated with the imperial religion. The Ephesian Olympic games were based on the Panhellenic Olympic games and were first held in ca. AD 90 in honor of Domitian[70] but lapsed after his disgrace till ca. AD 115 when it was likely held in honor of Hadrian.[71]

Ephesus had few ties with Olympian Zeus, concentrating instead on his twin children Artemis and Apollo but, in the second century AD, Hadrian would be hailed as Emperor Caesar Hadrian Zeus Olympus.[72] This built on, rather than rejected, the local religious tradition but rearranged the hierarchy of the gods and placed the emperor in a direct and superior relationship to Artemis, as did the terrace of the temple. Olympian religion was concerned with the preservation of the ancient ways and relationships under a proper hierarchy. Temples, games, priesthoods,

---

66. Friesen, *Twice Neokoros*, 114–15.

67. An ancient Greek wrestling school, an essential addition to a gymnasium in Greek athletics.

68. Friesen, *Twice Neokoros*, 124.

69. Friesen, *Twice Neokoros*, 123, 137.

70. Friesen, *Twice Neokoros*, 134.

71. Friesen, *Twice Neokoros*, 117–18. Of the seven uncovered inscriptions referring to Zeus Olympios, six are referring to Hadrian.

72. Friesen, *Twice Neokoros*, 118. This follows Domitian's lead. A coin shows Domitian's head on the obverse along with the inscription proclaiming him as emperor and god while the reverse shows Zeus Olympia holding in his right hand the statue of Artemis. Friesen, *Twice Neokoros*, 119. This goes far beyond the twice *neokoros* coin where both were equal.

5. OTHER PAGAN RELIGIONS

sacrifices, and reverence were more important than "emotional sincerity, assent to doctrines, or divine essence."[73] While we have no indication of what the ritual activity entailed,[74] we do know that the imperial cult was taken seriously. It was not just political ritual. In antiquity, all aspects of life, social, religious, economic, and political, were intricately intertwined.[75]

The temple of Sebastoi was Asia's third operating imperial temple at a time when all other provinces only had one.[76] In this, Asia was leading the empire in the path of emperor worship.[77] Did the Greeks believe the emperor was a god? There is no evidence of fulfilled prayer by any emperor, dead or alive[78] but there are records of intense religious experience associated with these gods. There is a letter from an association of Demetriasts in Ephesus to the proconsul of the province of Asia about AD 88–89. In the letter they made their request as follows, "Mysteries and sacrifices are performed each year in Ephesus, lord, to Demeter Karpophoros (fruit bringer) and Thesmophoros (law giver) and to the *Sebastoi* gods by *mystai*[79] with great purity and lawful customs together with the priestesses."[80] There are also inscriptions which show how thoroughly emperor worship infiltrated not just religions but also the associations.[81] One example was an association of "physicians who sacrifice to the ancestor Asclepios and to the *Sebastoi*."[82]

73. Friesen, *Twice Neokoros*, 166.
74. Friesen, *Twice Neokoros*, 142.
75. Harland, "Honours and Worship," 322.
76. Friesen, "Roman Emperors," 245.
77. It may well be that Revelation dates from this time and reflects this rise of emperor worship.
78. Arnold, *Ephesians*, 37.
79. Unfortunately, we do not know what these mysteries were.
80. Harland, "Honours and Worship," 331.
81. Harland says, "Out of about one hundred inscriptions relating to associations and guilds in Ephesus (I–III CE) over twenty pertain in some way either to worshiping or honoring the emperor in a private or public setting or to some direct or indirect contact with the emperor, imperial cult, or its functionaries." Harland, "Honours and Worship," 224.
82. Harland, "Honours and Worship," 330.

Ephesus gained the official title and exceptional honor of "twice *Neokoros*" in the AD 130s after the building of a temple to Hadrian (85 by 57 meters) on a drained swamp north of the Xystoi.[83] The city went even further when it gained the right to build temples to the brother emperors (and sworn enemies) Caracalla and Geta. While a new temple was built for Geta, Caracalla allowed his honor to be given to Artemis. Soon after Geta was killed by Caracalla any evidence of his worship was erased. With this change "Ephesus was thus officially twice *neokoros* for the emperors and once for Artemis, for a total of three." In AD 218, an unprecedented fourth imperial temple was built for Emperor Elagabalus. He was unpopular and was soon killed and, as before, all memory of him erased. The city reverted to thrice *neokoros*. In the mid-third century AD, the emperor Valerian and his son Gallienus built the fourth *neokoria*. The empire was at war, Valerian was captured by the Persians and all mention of *neokoria* ceased.[84]

Women in Ephesian Cults

In Asia Minor, women were more conspicuous in religious life than elsewhere.[85] They served an important role[86] in the religious life of Ephesus, sometimes even serving as priests. This is not surprising considering the role of the Amazons in founding the worship of Artemis Ephesia.[87] A number of these women were known to have held this office in their own right, without being

---

83. Van der Linder, *Artemis Ephesia*, 171.
84. Burrell, "Ephesus as Temple-Warden," para. 5.
85. Strelan, *Paul, Artemis, and the Jews*, 120.
86. In Asia Minor, twenty-eight women are known to have held the position of *pyrtanis* (a position of very high rank involving the finances and cultic life of the city) in eight cities in the first three centuries after Christ. Thirty-seven were *stephanephoroi* (positions of high public profile and prestige, if not much political clout) in seventeen cities over a five-century period, and eighteen women in fourteen different cities held the position of *agonothetis* (a position of responsibility for contests) in the first three centuries. Trebilco, *Jewish Communities*, 120–22.
87. Pausanias, *Descr.* 7.2.4.

5. OTHER PAGAN RELIGIONS

dependent on their husbands.[88] They were known to be involved in the sacrificial activities from ca. AD 45.[89] Women also served as priestesses in the Artemision and in the cult of Hestia Boulaia in the civic center. In the Imperial cult, 26 percent of the 138 known high priests were women.[90] This prominent role would have been noticed by Ephesian Jews and Christians.

Artemis, who consorted with women and as the huntress took many of the roles that were seen as male, represented life without being constrained by men.[91] The goddess brought the power of women into the realm of men and for men.[92] Greek women's status and honor frequently came with marriage and families so Artemis's role in preparing maidens for this role was very important.[93]

Demeter, who was the goddess of corn, also had a strong following in Ephesus.[94] The *Thesmophoria* was a three-day festival exclusive to married women which was intended to "promote the fertility and productivity of both women and cereals and to celebrate the procreative qualities of women." During this festival in which the women acted as virgins waiting to be married, they participated in things excluded to them in normal life.[95] In this festival they could organize a women's society, stay outside overnight, and perform private secret rituals which included the otherwise forbidden drinking of wine. They even organized women guards to keep men away.[96] The "wild" nature of this living is in stark contrast to their everyday married life, tamed, civilized, and domesticated.

Another cult essentially for women was that of Dionysus. Dionysus in Greek mythology drove the Amazons to find refuge

---

88. Strelan, *Paul, Artemis, and the Jews*, 55; Friesen, *Twice Neokoros*, 84–86.

89. Friesen, *Twice Neokoros*, 113.

90. White, "Urban Development," 58.

91. As her role was to prepare women for marriage she would have been seen as advantageous to men also.

92. Strelan, *Paul, Artemis, and the Jews*, 122.

93. Strelan, *Paul, Artemis, and the Jews*, 120.

94. Herodotus, *Hist.* 6.16.

95. Strelan, *Paul, Artemis, and the Jews*, 121.

96. Strelan, *Paul, Artemis, and the Jews*, 121.

with Artemis in Ephesus. This double god of life and death was both male and female, bringing the power of men into the realm of women.[97] He entered the underworld looking for his mother and came out with the gift of life and celebration.[98] This "twin to himself"[99] was a god of confusion and described, along with Apollo by Achilles Tatius as "the most violent of gods . . . who drive the soul towards madness."[100]

The festival of Dionysius, held in Ephesus's cold winter, turned the city into the wilds outside of the city. The women went about in bare feet and with hair unbraided and ate raw meat and drank wine. All of this suggests a trance-like state which climaxed in ecstasy.[101] By eating flesh and drinking wine the participants identified with the god.[102] This possession by the gods was arrived at through chanting, dancing, rhythmic drumming and cymbals and the music of flutes.[103]

The *katagogia* was a festival where the worshipers of Dionysus came down from the hills into the city. Women would come forward to be beaten with cudgels to promote fertility and commune with the dead.[104] Death and blood were powerful connections in the cult, and in this festival the participants would "die" and be at one with the god and so access his life-giving power.[105] There were some similarities in the religion of Dionysus to Christian claims. In the apocryphal *Acts of Timothy*, Timothy lost his life when opposing the *katagogia*.

Women had influence beyond these cults as well. In Plautus's (third century BC) Latin play *Miles Gloriosus*, an elderly Ephesian gentleman complained about wives who were always asking their

97. Strelan, *Paul, Artemis, and the Jews*, 122.
98. Strelan, *Paul, Artemis, and the Jews*, 122.
99. Aelius Aristides, *Orat.* 41.4–5.
100. Achilles Tatius, *Leuc. Clit.* 2.2.3.
101. Strelan, *Paul, Artemis, and the Jews*, 122.
102. Strelan, *Paul, Artemis, and the Jews*, 124,
103. Strelan, *Paul, Artemis, and the Jews*, 122.
104. Strelan, *Paul, Artemis, and the Jews*, 123–24.
105. Strelan, *Paul, Artemis, and the Jews*, 124.

5. OTHER PAGAN RELIGIONS

husbands for money to buy presents for their mothers at the matrons' festival (in honor of Mars or possibly Ares), or give to the sorcerer, or dream interpreter, or clairvoyant or the soothsayer.[106] All terms are female, and all women charged for their services. The situation for women in Ephesus has been summarized as:

> With Artemis they "belonged"—they were part of the city, its cult, its traditions, and its wealth; with Demeter, they were associated with the cycle of death and life, production and reproduction, and so had power (even magical) on the estates and outlying farms and gardens of the city, as they planted and nurtured crops; with Dionysus they were able to transgress the barriers between marriage and virginity, between male and female, between humans and the gods.[107]

Magic in Ephesus

Magic normally differs from religion in two ways. Firstly, it is a deviation from sanctioned religious practice and secondly the results are almost guaranteed.[108] Magic was generally practiced by the lower classes, so the magical papyri give an insight into the beliefs and fears of the common people in the Hellenistic world. Interest in and fear of supernatural power and the demonic realm gripped the inhabitants of the whole Hellenistic world in the first century AD. Western Asia Minor was the center of a flourishing magical trade.[109] It is not surprising that in the book bearing the name of the city,[110] there is a strong emphasis on the power of God contrasted with the powers of evil. The Devil and the various

---

106. Plautus, *Mil. glo.* 691–99. The play is also known as *The Braggart Captain*.
107. Strelan, *Paul, Artemis, and the Jews*, 125.
108. Arnold, *Ephesians*, 19.
109. Arnold, *Ephesians*, 5.
110. While there are arguments about who wrote Ephesians and from where, there is strong agreement that the epistle was written to western Asia Minor. It is likely to be a circular letter distributed from Ephesus.

powers of evil are mentioned sixteen times.[111] In Acts 19, Luke indicates that there was a substantial number of new Christians who had still been practicing magic. Books that were worth 50,000 days wages were burnt by the believers.[112]

The spirit world was seen to exercise influence over all aspects of life. The magician's role was to know which spirits were helpful and which were harmful and to know the operation, strengths, and authority of the spirits.[113] By knowing the right formula, power could be exerted for good, such as enhancing sexual passion or for ill through uttering a curse. The practitioners of this magic crossed all religious boundaries, calling on a variety of names showing Egyptian, Greek, and even Jewish influences.[114] In the first Century, an interest in the divine personalities in the Roman Empire would be superseded by an interest in divine power.[115] People took an active role towards receiving and being strengthened by this supernatural power to protect themselves from evil forces that could harm them or cause illnesses.[116]

The reputation of Ephesus as a magic center is linked to its association with the "Ephesian Letters." The "genuine" *Ephesia Grammata* were six magical terms[117] that were most likely associated with Ephesian Artemis and were considered the "the magical formula *par excellence* in the Hellenistic world."[118] The origin and meaning of these words is uncertain but they are known from as early as the fourth century BC and came to be applied to written magical spells. For pagans, they continued as powerful and living

---

111. Only 1 Cor has more references, but it is three times longer.
112. Arnold, *Ephesians*, 15.
113. Arnold, *Ephesians*, 18.
114. Arnold, *Ephesians*, 18.
115. Arnold, *Ephesians*, 34.
116. Arnold, *Ephesians*, 34–35.
117. These six words are likely to be regarded as persons as they are addressed directly as persons who are "beneficial, protecting spirits." McCown, "Ephesia Grammata," 135.
118. McCown, "Ephesia Grammata," 128.

5. OTHER PAGAN RELIGIONS

and beneficial spirits through to at least the fourth century AD.[119] These letters were either spoken as evil averting spells, charms, or written amulets[120] kept in little sewn bags and were seen to have power to ward off evil spirits.[121] The holder of these names had access to the supernatural power of the being named. Even the mere allusion to the names and warning the evil forces that they are known can be sufficient.[122]

As the Ephesia Grammata were written onto Ephesian Artemis's image, her power was given to them and to Hellenistic magic. After studying the magical papyri, one researcher concluded that:

> in many instances there seems to be little or no difference between calling on Artemis to accomplish a certain task and utilizing a 'magical' formula. Magic appears to be less a substructure of the cult of Artemis than it is an integral aspect of her "religion." The magical aspects of her cult ... would certainly not be viewed as unsanctioned or "illegal."[123]

Hellenistic magic in western Asia Minor was not exclusively linked to Artemis though as all known gods are named in the papyri. There was no real preference for a particular deity.[124]

Artemis is frequently linked to the underworld goddesses, Hekate (from Greece) and Ereshkigal (from Mesopotamia), confirming her own role as an underworld goddess.[125] The three are

119. McCown, "Ephesia Grammata," 139.

120. The magical documents from Asia Minor have not survived but, due to the dry climate, a number from Egypt have. It is thought that these would be substantially like the magic in Asia Minor. Arnold, *Ephesians*, 16. Strelan argues that there is no evidence for this. Strelan, *Paul, Artemis, and the Jews*, 82. However it seems reasonable especially as Ephesus was a great port with regular contact with Alexandria.

121. Arnold, *Ephesians*, 15.

122. McCown, "Ephesia Grammata," 132, 134–35.

123. Arnold, *Ephesians*, 24.

124. Arnold, *Ephesians*, 35.

125. Strelan argues that in Greek and presumably Ephesian thought a goddess of the underworld did not evoke fear and dread. Strelan, *Paul, Artemis, and the Jews*, 82.

seen as possessing the keys to Hades.[126] As the most powerful ghost goddess she had the power to deliver people from the spirits. Astrology is closely associated with magic because through it a person could alter his fate by manipulating the astral powers. Artemis, with the signs of the zodiac on her image, was unaffected by astrological fate and truly able to help her followers and give advice about the future.[127] The mystery religions were closely connected with astrology and, as mentioned already, the worship of Artemis Ephesia was also associated with the practice of mysteries. It offered a different way of gaining the favor of the evil heavenly powers.[128] In the mysteries of Cybele, which may have similarities to those of Ephesian Artemis, the blood of a slaughtered bull was drained through lattice work in the altar onto an initiate below. The strength of the beast was transferred to the person being,[129] in a sense, "baptised" and "washed in the blood." By adding to magic, astrology, and mysteries the three overlapped to make Artemis's cult very powerful by having complementary ways of manipulating the powers.[130]

Gnosticism

The term "gnostic" comes from the Greek, *ginosko*, "to know" or "understand." That is about how far agreement goes among scholars who try to define what it was/is[131] as a religious system. Some have very narrow definitions and others very broad. It has been said that "one man's Gnosticism may be simply another man's Mysticism, Esoterism, Docetism, or Encratism."[132] It is disputed by

    126. Arnold, *Ephesians*, 24.
    127. Arnold, *Ephesians*, 28.
    128. Arnold, *Ephesians*, 29.
    129. Arnold, *Ephesians*, 28.
    130. Arnold, *Ephesians*, 29.
    131. Some would see Gnosticism in the religiosity of the Rosicrucians, the freemasons, and Carl Jung. Yamauchi, *Pre-Christian Gnosticism*, 17.
    132. Yamauchi, *Pre-Christian Gnosticism*, 13. *Esoterism* involves possessing knowledge (often secret) that is held only by a limited number of people.

5. OTHER PAGAN RELIGIONS

those with a narrow definition whether this heresy existed in the first century[133] and scholars generally refer to proto-Gnosticism during this period.[134] Far from being a unified system it was a speculative religious belief with its teachers taking as they chose from Platonic philosophy, oriental mysticism, cabbalistic Judaism, and Christianity. Gnosticism took many varied forms, from gross immorality to a highly ethical life. This divergence was possible as salvation came from their inner spiritual nature, not by any ethical considerations.[135] However, Gnosticism, in its various forms, when fully developed was a heresy which was to plague the second-century church. A large part of the danger of their followers to the church was that many would call themselves "Christian" and were not always easy to tell from orthodox believers.[136]

This great variation has made it difficult to come to agreement on what Gnosticism even is. Gnostics were, however, united in their attempt to come to God by their own reasoning and in their rejection of the incarnation of Christ. Gnosticism taught that God was entirely separate from the creation and so contact was made through a series of intermediary beings called *demiurges*. This was necessary as matter was seen as inherently evil but the soul, however, was pure celestial element imprisoned by some tragic fate in a material body. This knowledge was "essentially saving knowledge, salvation is through self-acquaintance, and this knowledge tends to be reserved for the elite."[137]

Gnosticism's core was the "mystery religions which mediate secret knowledge leading to salvation and from magic whose knowledge confers supernatural powers and union with God.

Docetists would hold that Christ's body was not real but only a phantom. Therefore, his sufferings were only apparent. The followers of *Encratism* renounced marriage and abstained from meat and wine.

133. Arnold is adamant that no evidence exists for the existence of Gnosticism in first century Asia Minor. Arnold, *Ephesians*, 8.
134. Arnold, *Ephesians*, 7.
135. Logan, "Gnosticism," 914.
136. Justin, *1 Apol.* 1.26: Eusebius, *Hist. eccl.* 2.1.2; 2.13.6–8.
137. Logan, "Gnosticism," 907.

97

This was nothing new to the Ephesians as there were mysteries associated with the worship of Artemis. Gnosticism was set in the framework of contemporary philosophy, mythology and astrology and later Christianity."[138] The gnostics were concerned with ultimate salvation and differed from magic, which was about systematizing, understanding, and manipulating the supernatural for a present benefit.[139]

While Christianity and Gnosticism emerged on the scene at about the same time, they are distinct religions though some argue the latter is derived from the former.[140] The church fathers unanimously claimed Simon Magus from Gitta, a pagan area of Samaria was the arch-gnostic though Luke only refers to him as a magician (Acts 8:9–24). He went to Rome under Claudius accompanied by a prostitute from Tyre called Helen who he called his *Ennoia* (first thought). He considered himself to be a god and that this "Thought" leaped forth from him in the beginning and generated the angels who made the world. Helen was then seized by the angels and held captive in various bodies down the ages (Helen of Troy, and the "lost sheep" of the Gospels) until appearing as a common prostitute. Simon came in the form of a man to save her and to offer salvation through his knowledge. He would appear to the Jews as Son, to the Samarians as Father and the nations as Holy Spirit.[141] Two things separated Simon from later Gnosticism though: Simon claimed to be divine and salvation came from recognizing him, not through any self-knowledge.[142]

---

138. Because of gnostic tendencies that existed in the first century, a limited agreement has developed between those who accept and those who deny Pauline authorship of the Pastoral Epistles. Towner, "Gnosis," 96. The heresy in the Pastorals is said to be, if not full-blown Gnosticism, at least an early form of Gnosticism originating in Christians with a Hellenistic Jewish background who merged the associated beliefs into orthodox Christianity. There are also close similarities with the Hellenistic Judaism found in Colossae (Col 2:3–8, 16–23).

139. Arnold, *Ephesians*, 11.

140. Yamauchi, *Pre-Christian Gnosticism*, 21.

141. Irenaeus, *Haer.* 1.23.1–5; Justin, *1 Apol.* 1.26.

142. Yamauchi, *Pre-Christian Gnosticism*, 62.

5. OTHER PAGAN RELIGIONS

Ephesus was a center for early Gnosticism and Cerinthus (died ca. AD 100), who was trained in Egypt and probably reared a Jew,[143] is the person associated with it. Hippolytus in his *Refutation of all Heresies* wrote of Cerinthus saying that he alleged:

> That, after the baptism (of our Lord), Christ in form of a dove came down upon him, from that absolute sovereignty which is above all things. And then, (according to this heretic,) Jesus proceeded to preach the unknown father, and in attestation (of his mission) to work miracles. It was, however, (the opinion of Cerinthus,) that ultimately Christ departed from Jesus, and that Jesus suffered and rose again, whereas that Christ, being spiritual, remained beyond the possibility of suffering.[144]

Polycarp, a disciple of John, remembered an occurrence when the apostle came across Cerinthus. The apostle believed Cerinthus's message was so hostile to Christianity that, as Polycarp recounted, "John, the disciple of the Lord, (was) going to bathe at Ephesus, and perceiving Cerinthus within, rushed out of the bathhouse without bathing, exclaiming, 'Let us fly, lest even the bath-house fall down, because Cerinthus, the enemy of the truth, is within.'"[145]

---

143. Elwell and Comfort, *Dictionary*, s.v. "Ephesus."
144. Hippolytus, *Haer.* 5.21.
145. Irenaeus, *Haer.* 3.3.4.

6. Judaism and Christianity in Ephesus

Judaism

JEWS LIVED IN EPHESUS from the early Hellenistic period[1] and there was a large Jewish population in Asia Minor throughout the Hellenistic and Roman periods. Antiochus III (ca. 241–187 BC) had moved 2000 Jewish families from Mesopotamia to Asia Minor to secure his hold there.[2] It is thought that by imperial times, as much as 10% of the population of a Greco-Roman city could be Jewish meaning there could be upwards of 25,000 Jews in the Ephesus in New Testament times.[3] Three classical authors wrote about the Jews of Asia Minor in the first century BC, but their works have all been lost.[4] Fortunately, Josephus sheds considerable light on the very strong Jewish presence in Ionia, with at least twelve references to Ephesus in his writings.

The Jew's religion was protected by the Seleucids[5] and later the Romans[6] who accepted and defined their position on an ad hoc basis. The Jews were given the right to be organized into a community, freely assemble [7] and follow their religion, to observe their Sabbath and holy days, not be involved in military service, and to

1. Josephus, *Ag. Ap.* 2.4.
2. Safrai and Stern, *Jewish People*, 1:152.
3. Strelan, *Paul, Artemis, and the Jews*, 181.
4. Trebilco, *Jewish Communities*, 19.
5. Josephus, *Ant.* 14.10.22.
6. Josephus, *Ant.* 14.10.23–5; 16.6.1.
7. Josephus, *Ant.* 14.10.8.

6. JUDAISM AND CHRISTIANITY IN EPHESUS

have money in Jerusalem as well as "sacred money."[8] Support for the Jews by Rome in Asia Minor was because:

- It followed the precedent of their predecessors,
- It showed gratitude and mutual esteem between leaders (Hyrcanus II and Julius Caesar[9] and Marcus Agrippa and Herod),
- Toleration was an important part of Roman rule, and
- It helped gain the support of the Jews and avoided unrest.[10]

There was no significant support by the Jews of Asia Minor for the Jewish revolt in Palestine (AD 66–70) and the wider revolt in Egypt, Cyrenaica, Cyprus, and Mesopotamia (AD 115–17). Because of this the Roman government continued the privileged position of the Jews of Asia Minor despite requests to the contrary by various cities.[11] These privileges continued under the Christian emperors.

We know from Josephus that these freedoms could be abused or totally ignored by the Ionian Greeks. Litigation against Jews could be scheduled for the Sabbath.[12] As well their sacred money could be interfered with.[13] The pagan Greeks were intolerant of a religious system that was both very strange to them and for the special privileges the Jews experienced. The excuse given for this was that "the Jews inhabited in their country, they were entirely unjust to them [in not joining in their worship] but they demonstrated their

---

8. Josephus, *Ant.* 16.6.1–7.
9. Josephus, *Ant.* 14.7.
10. Trebilco, *Jewish Communities*, 11.
11. Trebilco, *Jewish Communities*, 32.
12. Josephus, *Ant.* 16.6.1–7.
13. This could be an issue if the region was experiencing economic difficulties given the large amount of money involved. Josephus quotes Strabo as saying that Mithridates stole 800 talents which belonged to the Jews and was being stored at Cos for safety. Josephus, *Ant.* 14.13.113.

generosity in this, that though they worshipped according to their institutions, they did nothing that ought to grieve them."[14]

Jews had a very different attitude to membership of a community than did the Greeks. The Talmud said that a Jew could consider himself a member of the community after he had lived in it for a year or purchased a house.[15] This modern view of the Jews is in striking contrast to the Greeks which remained fundamentally tribal.[16] The Greeks considered membership of a *polis* as an exclusive privilege deriving from an hereditary position or by a special grant by the city.[17] A considerable amount is known about the citizenship of Jews in another Hellenistic city, Alexandria, but it does not follow that the same situation applied in Asia Minor. The most probable situation is that they possessed *isopoliteia*, the status of potential citizenship. This could be validated at any time by participation in the pagan rites.[18] Despite not having formal citizenship there were collective rights enjoyed by the community.[19]

Whereas the trades were generally closed to newcomers through the guild system, there was a remarkable openness among the Jewish craftsmen in the first-century Jewish communities.[20] This reception would have strengthened and promoted the growth of their communities.[21] Judea itself dominated the trade in very profitable luxury goods coming from Africa via the Red Sea or the Orient and Arabia via Petra.[22] The cities in Asia Minor were forced to accept these goods from Judean harbors presumably with Jewish middle men. It has been suggested that this was "one of the

---

14. Josephus, *Ant.* 16.2.4.
15. Safrai and Stern, *Jewish People*, 2:434.
16. Safrai and Stern, *Jewish People*, 2:434.
17. Safrai and Stern, *Jewish People*, 2:434.
18. Safrai and Stern, *Jewish People*, 2:438.
19. Safrai and Stern, *Jewish People*, 2:439.
20. Safrai and Stern, *Jewish People*, 2:482.
21. Consider the relationship of Aquila of Pontus and Paul of Tarsus who worked together in the same trade (Acts 18:3).
22. Safrai and Stern, *Jewish People*, 2:482.

6. JUDAISM AND CHRISTIANITY IN EPHESUS

main causes for political anti-Semitism manifested by the Greek cities of Asia in the second half of the first century."[23]

Josephus shows a community of Jews in Asia Minor which maintained a concern for matters that were at the heart of their faith, and which protected their Jewish identity. They were known to have built synagogues and the sanctity of their scriptures was ensured by Rome.[24] The temple tax (a half shekel or two denarii) was paid by every male and shipped to Jerusalem showing a continued loyalty to Jerusalem and the temple worship. This tax was granted the same sanctity as that of a pagan temple. In Agrippa's decree to the Ephesians,[25] people who stole this tax were deemed to have despoiled a temple and were not eligible to the right of sanctuary in the temple.[26] Jews in Asia Minor from 43 BC were exempt from conscription into the army in emergencies[27] because it conflicted with the Sabbath observance and dietary requirements of the law. The observance of the Sabbath by the Jews was so strong that, as previously mentioned, their opponents scheduled court hearings for the Sabbath, so the Jews found themselves having to choose between Sabbath observance and justice. The decree to Sardis stipulated that the city was to ensure that suitable food was to be available to the Jews, indicating that the Jews of Asia Minor were able to satisfy their food laws.[28]

Despite their Sabbath being given over to the study of the law[29] and Paul's first Ephesian ministry being in a synagogue (Acts 18:19), no synagogue has yet to be unearthed. As well, "there is a dearth of evidence, (e.g., lamps) and of inscriptional evidence as to the presence of Ephesian Judaism in the Greco-Roman era."[30]

---

23. Safrai and Stern, *Jewish People*, 2:668.
24. Josephus, *Ant.* 16.6.2.
25. Josephus, *Ant.* 16.2.4.
26. Josephus, *Ant.* 16.6.2.
27. Trebilco, *Jewish Communities*, 17.
28. Josephus, *Ant.* 14.10.24.
29. Josephus, *Ant.* 16.2.3.
30. Oster, "Ephesus," 549.

Table 1 shows what to us would be a very confusing religious scene with initially only the Jews standing apart from all this. When Christianity appeared on the scene it would have been seen by outsiders as just another religion competing for the hearts and minds of the citizens. Christianity and Judaism were both different as they demanded the sole allegiance of the believer. The Greek and Roman understanding did not demand this exclusivity. There was no problem worshiping one then another of the Greek or Roman pantheon or for that matter even participating in totally different unrelated religions.

The Jews proved to be zealous defenders of the law and the temple and opposed Christianity with its preaching of a gospel without the law. Yet both groups would be looked on by the pagans as atheists because of their monotheism.[31]

Christianity

To the Ephesian pagans, Christianity was just another new arrival among the plethora of foreign gods and initially would not have caused any concern. All that was required was for Jesus to be jointly worshiped with Artemis or the other gods, but this was not going to happen. The New Testament period can be divided into two, the first centered on the ministry of Paul and the second on John. During the second missionary journey, Paul, accompanied by Silas and Timothy passed near to Ephesus but were prevented by the Holy Spirit from preaching in the city (Acts 16:6). At the end of the same journey (ca. AD 52), Paul passed through the city, leaving Priscilla and Aquila to minister there (Acts 18:18–19). Paul's friends found an Alexandrian called Apollos, who, despite teaching accurately about Jesus, only knew John's baptism. Paul later returned and ministered in Ephesus for about two years (ca. AD 52–55), the longest period he is known to have spent in ministry in one location. Paul also found believers in

---

31. Harland, "Christ-Bearers," 499. Polycarp, Bishop of Smyrna (69–155) was martyred, accused of the charge of atheism. *Martyrdom of Polycarp*, 3.2, 9.2.

6. JUDAISM AND CHRISTIANITY IN EPHESUS

Christ that practiced John's baptism and who had not heard of the Holy Spirit (Acts 19:2-4). Twenty years after Christ's death it was possible to find a mixture of accuracy and error when it came to understanding the gospel.

Paul's two-year ministry was characterized by powerful preaching (Acts 19:8) and outstanding miracles (Acts 19:11-12) which were accompanied by numerous conversions. This led to a remarkable change in the believers as they abandoned their old polytheist ways (Acts 19:18-19). Paul must have used Ephesus as a base of operations for spreading the gospel to nearby cities and throughout Asia Minor. The apostle's opponents would say he had led astray many people here and in the whole province of Asia (Acts 19:26). The church was built, and church government was established (Acts 20:17). His stay in Ephesus experienced strong opposition, first from the Jews but more strongly from the followers of Artemis. Luke describes a vivid confrontation between a mob at fever pitch in the arena defending Artemis against the newcomers. The dangers were real and those with vested interests such as the silversmiths were able to play to the residents' role as *Neokoros* of Artemis (Acts 19:23-41). All prospered from the trade she brought. Luke's account in 1 Cor 15:32 of Paul fighting with wild beasts in Ephesus speaks to the intensity of the opposition. But alongside this, Paul also found favor at the highest level of Ephesian Society with the Asiarchs (Acts 19:31).

Around ca. AD 57 Paul passed by Ephesus and met the elders and predicted that, from among them, some would arise and damage the church. He went on to prison in Caesarea and Rome but contrary to expectation appears to have arrived in Ephesus again ca. 62.[32] He left Timothy behind to sort out matters in the church. By the time of Timothy's ministry, the church in Ephesus was in trouble, but not in the full-blown heresy that Paul had predicted in Acts 20 and 1 Tim 4:1. Tradition,[33] though not as well attested

---

32. This assumes that Paul was released from prison in Rome and made a fourth missionary journey.

33. The majority of second-century Christian authors say that John ministered in Ephesus at the end of the first century but there is not universal

105

EPHESUS: THE NURSERY OF CHRISTIANITY

as for Paul, says that John (and perhaps Mary) lived to an old age and eventually died in Ephesus. Though there is no direct biblical evidence he may have written his Gospel and epistles for this city. Perhaps another twenty years on from Timothy's ministry, this long-predicted falling away would happen during the time John was there. The name of the heretic is known: Cerinthus. The church would survive Cerinthus as he and his followers went out from among them (1 John 2:18–19).

The last reference to Ephesus in the Bible is found in the warnings to the seven churches (Rev 2:1–7). While the date of Revelation is disputed it was probably towards the end of Domitian's reign (AD 81–96). The church in Ephesus was approved for its hard work, perseverance, discernment, and endurance. Despite suffering so much, they had not grown weary, but they had lost their first love—seemingly contradictory. If they did not change their way the church was in danger of dying but, in their favor, was the fact that they could not tolerate the work of wicked men, particularly the Nicolaitans.

Papias refers to two Johns, one who was in the company of the Lord's disciples, and another who is in another group and described as "the presbyter."[34] Eusebius comments that "This shows that the statement of those is true, who say that there were two persons in Asia that bore the same name, and that there were two tombs in Ephesus, each of which, even to the present day, is called John's tomb. It is important to notice this. For it is probable that it was the second, if one is not willing to admit that it was the first that saw the Revelation, which is ascribed by name to John."[35] These two Johns have given rise to many alternative theories about the writers of the Gospel and the Revelation.[36]

---

agreement. Herman Koester makes a case for the apostle John never going to Ephesus, but Raymond Brown assesses the evidence that John was at Ephesus as impressive. Koester, "Ephesus," 135–139; Brown, *John*, lxxxix.

34. Eusebius, *Hist. eccl.* 34.4.

35. Eusebius, *Hist. eccl.* 34.6.

36. Koester is adamant that John the presbyter is the writer of the Revelation. Koester, "Ephesus," 137.

6. JUDAISM AND CHRISTIANITY IN EPHESUS

In the second century, Ignatius, Bishop of Antioch, while traveling as a prisoner through Asia Minor to martyrdom in Rome ca. AD 110, wrote a letter to this church. It stresses the need for unity[37] and to guard against false teachers. Ignatius refers to the Ephesians as fellow imitators of Paul.[38] He makes no mention of John but spoke of a bishop, Onesimus, suggesting a much more advanced system of church government. He calls the church to be like a choral group in a temple "attuned to the bishop as strings to the lyre."[39] Both Paul (1 Cor 15) and Ignatius drew on what was publicly known about the mystery religions to speak to the Christians in Asia Minor. He used language that a polytheistic audience would be familiar with. The Christian mystery included the virgin birth, actual raising of the dead and the mystery of the coming of the Lord.[40] Ignatius called the members of the Ephesian church fellow initiates of the gospel with Paul[41] and image bearers of God and Christ,[42] alluding to the frequent processions in the city.

Justin Martyr[43] (ca. AD 100–165) was also associated with the city in the first half of that century as he was thought to have been converted there and was known to be teaching the faith in Ephesus in the AD 130s. Though his First Apology was written from Rome, the description of a Christian worship service is not likely to have been any different from that which occurred in Ephesus:

> And on the day called Sunday, all who live in cities or in the country gather together to one place, and the memoirs of the apostles or the writings of the prophets are read, as long as time permits; then, when the reader

37. Ignatius *Eph.* 3:2; 4:5.
38. Ignatius *Eph.* 12.2.
39. Ignatius *Eph.* 4.
40. Ignatius *Eph.* 19.1–3.
41. Ignatius, *Eph.* 12.3.
42. Ignatius, *Eph.* 9.2.

43. Justin was formerly a philosopher and after his conversion he dressed as a philosopher and taught that the Logos acted in history before the incarnation of Christ, planting "seeds of Christianity." He would claim that some Greek philosophers, which included Socrates and Plato, were "unknowing Christians."

has ceased, the president verbally instructs, and exhorts to the imitation of these good things. Then we all rise together and pray, and, as we before said, when our prayer is ended, bread and wine and water are brought, and the president in like manner offers prayers and thanksgivings, according to his ability, and the people assent, saying Amen; and there is a distribution to each, and a participation of that over which thanks have been given, and to those who are absent a portion is sent by the deacons. And they who are well to do, and willing, give what each thinks fit; and what is collected is deposited with the president, who succours the orphans and widows and those who, through sickness or any other cause, are in want, and those who are in bonds and the strangers sojourning among us, and in a word takes care of all who are in need. But Sunday is the day on which we all hold our common assembly, because it is the first day on which God, having wrought a change in the darkness and matter, made the world; and Jesus Christ our Saviour on the same day rose from the dead. For He was crucified on the day before that of Saturn (Saturday); and on the day after that of Saturn, which is the day of the Sun, having appeared to His apostles and disciples.[44]

When Artemis failed to deliver her part in the salvation of the city and proved unable to protect her house or treasure, the whole natural order of interdependence of the human and the divine in a hierarchical society was challenged. In its place would come, at least ideally, a more:

> vertical and centralized society, . . . based on the generosity of an all-powerful giver. The ultimate act of generosity by that giver had been God's *synkatabasis* ("condescension"): sending his son down to earth. Such a giver, it must be obvious, had no need of mortal saviors, however rich they might be. Nor was the saving grace of Christ given on the basis of human actions, such as building fountains or gymnasia.[45]

44. Justin, *1 Apol.* 67.
45. Rogers, *Mysteries of Artemis*, 283–84.

6. JUDAISM AND CHRISTIANITY IN EPHESUS

The Basilica of St John built in the sixth century by Justinian over what was believed to be the grave of the apostle John

Three church councils were held in Ephesus in the years AD 431, 449, and 475. The first of these is regarded as the third ecumenical council where it was aimed to achieve consensus among the church. The others do not have this status. Ephesus I confirmed the Nicaean Creed and condemned the teaching of Nestorius, the Patriarch of Constantinople, who taught that Mary could be called *Christotokos*, "Christ-bearer," but not the *Theotokos*, "God-bearer." In the fifth and sixth century a popular site grew up of Mary the Theotokos, "she who gave birth to God." There, the story of Mary nursing Jesus, the powerful God who was both human and divine, was celebrated. The Ephesians were connected again to a story of a mother who gave birth to a deity.

The warnings to the seven churches in Rev 1–3 included a warning that the church in Ephesus would cease to exist (2:4–6) if it did not repent. The church did not survive the onslaught of Islam as was foretold. Today there is only a very small church in Selcuk, the modern town, and 99 percent of the population of Turkey are Muslims.

Conclusion

THE GREAT PORT OF Ephesus has now silted and is located kilometers from the sea. Kings and emperors that tried to tell the inhabitants who their savior was, and how she was to be worshiped, have long turned to dust. As for Artemis, she likewise has gone from local memory along with the ruins of her once great temple which had sunk six meters below the surface of the swamp on which it was built.

While the ruins are just a tourist attraction, and her temple site is normally just a stagnant pond inhabited by frogs, the legacy of this once great city lives on in our New Testament. Modern men and women still take comfort, advice, and correction from the struggles of a minority trying to live a new and foreign faith in a pagan and at times hostile community and government.

Source of Illustrations

Title	Source
Location of Ephesus	Author
Aerial view of Ephesus harbor	OeAW-OeAI/Niki Gail
Silver Tetradrachm	Macquarie University, *The Coinage of Ephesus*. Used with permission.
Temple of Hadrian	Shutterstock.
Division of Alexander's empire	Author
Portrait head of Lysimachus	José Luiz Bernardes Ribeiro
Layout of Roman Ephesus	OeAI-OeAW/C. Kurtze
Views of the commercial Agora	Shutterstock.
The theater in Ephesus	Shutterstock.
Roman Era Aqueduct	Dan Kistler. Used with permission.
Classical Greek Artemis	Shutterstock.
Artemis Ephesia	Shutterstock
Temple site	Shutterstock
Wood's reconstruction of the temple	Macquarie University, *The Coinage of Ephesus*. Used with permission.

SOURCE OF ILLUSTRATIONS

Title	Source
Column base in the British Museum	Lisa Weichel. Used with permission
Septimius Severus coin	Macquarie University, *The Coinage of Ephesus*. Used with permission.
Market at the base of the Imperial temple	Shutterstock.
Basilica of St John	Ricardo Sanchez Vicent

Bibliography

Aelian. *Historical Miscellany*. Translated by N. G. Wilson. Cambridge: Harvard University Press, 1997.
———. "On the Nature of Animals." In *On Animals*, translated by A. F. Scholfield, 3:157–212. 3 vols. London: Heinemann, 1959.
Antipater of Sidon. "Epigrams." In *Greek Anthology*, translated by W. R. Paton, 3:31. London: Heineman, 1943.
Appian. *The Foreign Wars*. Translated by Horace White. New York: Macmillan 1899.
Apuleius, Lucius. "The Golden Ass." Translated by A. S. Kline. https://www.poetryintranslation.com/PITBR/Latin/TheGoldenAssXI.php#anchor_Toc353982292.
Aristides, P. Aelius. *Aelius Aristides, the Complete Works: Volume 1, Panathenaic Oration, in Defence of Oratory*. Translated by Charles A. Behr. Leiden: Brill, 1981.
Arnold, Clinton E. *Ephesians: Power and Magic, the Concept of Power in Ephesians in Light of Its Historical Setting*. Cambridge: Cambridge University Press, 1989.
———. "Ephesus." In *Dictionary of Paul and His Letters*, edited by Gerald F. Hawthorne and Ralph P. Martin, 249–53. Downers Grove: InterVarsity, 1993.
Arnold, Irene Ringwood. "Festivals of Ephesus." *American Journal of Archaeology* 76.1 (1972) 17–22.
Arrian. *The Anabasis of Alexander*. Translated by E. J. Chinnock. London: Hodder & Stoughton, 1884.
Athenaeus. *The Deipnosophists, Volume 4*. Translated by Charles Burton Gulick. Cambridge: Harvard University Press, 1959.
Augustus Caesar. *The Deeds of Divine Augustus*. http://classics.mit.edu/Augustus/deeds.html.
Austrian Archaeological Institute. "Ephesos: Periurban Research." https://www.oeaw.ac.at/en/oeai/research/historical-archaeology/historical-archaeology-in-the-mediterranean/ephesos-periurban-research.
Baugh, S. M. "The Apostle Among the Amazons." *Westminster Theological Journal* 56 (1994) 154–172.

BIBLIOGRAPHY

―――. "Cult Prostitution in New Testament Ephesus: A Reappraisal." *Journal of the Evangelical Theological Society* 42.3 (1999) 443–60.

―――. "A Foreign World, Ephesus in the First Century." In *Women in the Church: An Interpretation and Application of 1 Timothy 2:9–15*, edited by Andreas J Kostenberger and Thomas R Schreiner, 25–64. Wheaton: Crossway, 2016.

Blaiklock, Edward M. "Ephesus." In *New International Dictionary of Biblical Archaeology*, edited by Edward M. Blaiklock and R. K. Harrison, 181. Grand Rapids: Zondervan, 1982.

Brenk, Frederick E. "Artemis of Ephesos: An Avant Garde Goddess." *Kernos Revue Internationale et Pluridisciplinaire de Religion Grecque Antique* 11 (1998) 157–71.

Brown, Raymond E. *The Gospel According to John I–XII.* Anchor Bible Series 29. New York: Doubleday, 1966.

―――. *An Introduction to the New Testament.* New York: Doubleday, 1997.

Burrell, Barbara. "The Bee and the Deer." https://www.mq.edu.au/research/research-centres-groups-and-facilities/resilient-societies/centres/australian-centre-for-ancient-numismatic-studies/exhibitions/the-coinage-of-ephesus/the-bee-and-the-deer.

Callimachus. "Hymns." *Callimachus: Hymns, Epigrams, Select Fragments*, translated by Stanley Lombado and Diane Raynor, 3–40. Baltimore: John Hopkins University Press, 1988.

Cassius Dio Cocceianus. *Dio's Roman History 6.* Translated by Earnest Cary. London: Heinemann, 1955.

―――. *Dio's Roman History 7.* Translated by Earnest Cary. London: Heinemann, 1960.

Crouch, D. P., and Ch. Ortloff. *Ephesus Municipal Water System Analysis.* https://web.archive.org/web/20210624205007/https://homepage.univie.ac.at/elisabeth.trinkl/forum/forum1297/05wass.htm.

Deligiannakis, Georgios. "Religious Viewing of Sculptural Images of Gods in the World of Late Antiquity: From Dio Chrysostom to Damaskios." *Journal of Late Antiquity* 8:1 (2015) 168-194.

Demosthenes, "Against Neaira." In *Orations (50–58), Private Cases in Nearam (59)*, translated by A. T. Murray, 6:350–453. Cambridge: Harvard University Press, 1939.

Dio Chrysostom. "The Thirty-First Discourse to the People of Rhodes." In *Dio Chrysostom*, translated by J. W. Cohoon and H. Lamar Crosby, 3:2–170. London: Heinemann, 1951.

Diodorus Siculus. *Diodorus of Sicily, Volume 10.* Translated by Russell M. Geer. Cambridge: Harvard University Press, 1954.

Duris of Elaea. "Declamatory Epigram 9.424." In *Greek Anthology*, translated by W. R. Paton, 3:235. London: William Heinemann, 1925.

Elwell, W. A., and P. W. Comfort. *Tyndale Bible Dictionary.* Wheaton: Tyndale House, 2001.

BIBLIOGRAPHY

"Ephesus." https://www.universiteitleiden.nl/en/research/research-projects/arch aeology/ephesus.
Eusebius. "Ecclesiastical History." In *The Nicene and Post-Nicene Fathers, Second Series: Eusebius: Church History, Life of Constantine the Great, and Oration in Praise of Constantine*, edited by Philip Schaff and Henry Wace, 1:81–386. New York: Christian Literature, 1890.
Falconer, W. "Preface." In *The Geography of Strabo*, translated by H. C. Hamilton and W. Falconer, 3:vi–xxvi. 3 vols. London: Bohn, 1857.
Fox, Robin L. *Alexander the Great*. London: Folio Society, 1997.
Friesen, Steven J. "The Cult of the Roman Emperors in Ephesos: Temple Wardens, City Titles, and the Interpretation of the Revelation of John." In *Ephesos, Metropolis of Asia*, 229–50. Valley Forge: Harvard Theological Studies, 1995.
———. *Twice Neokoros: Ephesus, Asia and the Cult of the Flavian Imperial Policy*. Leiden: Brill, 1993.
Frontinus, Sextus Julius. "Strategems." In *Stratagems: Aqueducts of Rome*, translated by Charles E. Bennett, 3–327. Cambridge: Harvard University Press, 1925.
Gill, Malcolm. *Jesus as Mediator*. Oxford: Lang, 2008.
Goodspeed, E. J. *New Chapters in New Testament Study*. New York, Macmillan, 1937.
Graves, Robert. *The Greek Myths: Volume 1*. London: Folio Society, 1996.
Greenhalgh, Michael. *The Greek and Roman Cities of Western Turkey*. http://rubens.anu.edu.au/raider4/turkey/turkeybook/intro1.html.
Gritz, Sharon H. *Paul, Women Teachers, and the Mother Goddess at Ephesus*. Lanham: University Press of America, 1991.
Harland, Philip A. "Christ-Bearers and Fellow-Initiates: Local Cultural Life and Christian Identity in Ignatius' Letters." *Journal of Early Christian Studies* 11.4 (2003) 481–99.
———. "Honours and Worship: Emperors, Imperial Cults and Associations at Ephesus (First to Third centuries C.e.)" *Studies in Religion/Sciences religieuses* 25 (1996) 319–34.
Herodotus. *The Histories*. Translated by Aubrey De Selincourt. Hammondsworth: Penguin, 1954.
Hesiod. "The Homeric Hymns." In *Works of Hesiod and the Homeric Hymns*, translated by Darryl Hine, 95–196. Chicago: Chicago University Press, 2005.
———. "Theogony." In *The Homeric Hymns and Homerica*, translated by Hugh G. Evelyn-White, 78–153. Cambridge: Harvard University Press, 1914.
Hippolytus. "Refutation of All Heresies." In *The Ante-Nicene Fathers, Volume 5: Hippolytus, Cyprian, Novatian, Appendix*, edited by A. Roberts et al., 9–162. Edinburgh: T. & T. Clark, 1885.
Hjerrild, Rodil. "Near Eastern Equivalents to Artemis." In *Acta Hyperborea*, edited by Tobias Fischer-Hansen and Birte Poulsen, 42–69. Copenhagen: Museum Tusculanum, 2009.

BIBLIOGRAPHY

Homer. *The Iliad in Two Volumes*. Translated by A. T. Murray. Cambridge: Harvard University Press, 1924.

Hooker, Morna D. "Artemis of Ephesus." *The Journal of Theological Studies* 64.1 (2013) 37–46.

Ignatius. "To the Ephesians." In *The Ante-Nicene Fathers: The Apostolic Fathers, Justin Martyr, Irenaeus*, edited by A. Roberts et al., 1:45–48. Edinburgh: T. & T. Clark, 1885.

Irenaeus. "Against Heresies." In *The Ante-Nicene Fathers: The Apostolic Fathers, Justin Martyr, Irenaeus*, edited by A. Roberts et al., 1:309–567. Edinburgh: T. & T. Clark, 1885.

Isocrates. *Isocrates with an English Translation in Three Volumes*. Translated by George Norlin. Cambridge: Harvard University Press, 1980.

Josephus, Flavius. *Complete Works*. Translated William Whinston. London: Pickering and Inglis, 1960.

Justin Martyr. "The First Apology of Justin." In *The Ante-Nicene Fathers: The Apostolic Fathers, Justin Martyr, Irenaeus*, edited by A. Roberts et al., 1:163–87. Edinburgh: T. & T. Clark, 1885.

Juvenal. "Satires." In *Juvenal and Persius*, translated by Susanna M. Braune, 128–512. Cambridge: Harvard University Press, 2004.

Knibbe, Dieter. "Via Sacra Ephesiaca: New Aspects of the Cult of Artemis Ephesia." In *Ephesos, Metropolis of Asia*, 141–56. Valley Forge: Harvard Theological Studies, 1995.

Koester, Craig R. "Roman Slave Trade and the Critique of Babylon in Revelation 18." *The Catholic Biblical Quarterly* 70.4 (2008) 766–86.

Koester, Herman. "Ephesus in Early Christian Literature." In *Ephesos, Metropolis of Asia*, 119–40. Valley Forge: Harvard Theological Studies, 1995.

LiDonnici, Lynn R. "The Image of Artemis Ephesia in Greco-Roman Worship: A Reconstruction." *Harvard Theological Review* 85.4 (1992) 389–415.

Logan, Alastair H. B. "Gnosticism." In *The Early Christian World*, edited by Philip F. Esler, 907–28. London: Routledge, 2002.

Magyar, Z. "Imperial Cult and Christianity: How and to What Extent Were the Imperial Cult and Emperor Worship Thought to Preserve Stability in The Roman World?" *Acta Archaeologica Academiae Scientiarum Hung* 60 (2009) 385–39.

Martin, Luther. *Hellenistic Religions: An Introduction*. Oxford: Oxford University Press, 1987.

"The Martyrdom of Polycarp." In *The Apostolic Fathers*, 2:309–45. 2 vols. London: Heinemann, 1913.

McCown, Chester C. "The Ephesia Gramamata in Popular Belief." *Transactions and Proceedings of the American Philological Association* 54 (1923) 128–140.

McDonald, L. M. "Ephesus." In *Dictionary of New Testament Background*, edited by Craig A Evans and Stanley E. Porter, 318–21. Downers Grove: InterVarsity, 2000.

BIBLIOGRAPHY

Mitchell, Stephen. *Anatolia: Land, Men, and Gods in Asia Minor*. 2 vols. Oxford: Clarendon, 1993.
Muss, Ulrike. "The Artemision in Early Christian Times." *Early Christianity* 7 (2016) 293–312.
———. "The Temple of Artemis and the Apostle Paul." *Sacred History Magazine* 7.1 (2011) 30–33.
Oster, Richard E. "The Ephesian Artemis as an Opponent of Early Christianity." *Jahrbuch für Antike und Christentum* 19 (1976) 24–44.
———. "Ephesus." In *The Anchor Bible Dictionary: D–G*, edited by David N. Freedman, 2:542–49. New York: Doubleday, 1992.
Pausanias. *Description of Greece*. Translated by J. G. Frazer. 6 vols. Loeb Classical Library. New York: Biblo and Tannen, 1965.
Payne, Philip B. "Liberterian Women in Ephesus: A Response to Douglas J. Moo's Article, '1 Timothy 2:11–15: Meaning and Signifigance.'" *Trinity Journal* 2 (1981) 170–98.
Philostratus the Elder. "Imagines." In *Philostratus Imagines, Callistatus Descriptions*, translated by Arthur Fairbanks, 3–282. London: Heinemann, 1931.
Philostratus the Athenian. *The Life of Apollonius of Tyana, Volume 1*. Translated by Christopher P. Jones. Cambridge: Harvard University Press, 2005.
———. "Life of the Sophists." In *Philostratus and Eunapius*, translated by Wilmer C. Wright, 4–318. Loeb Classical Library. London: William Heinemann, 1952.
Plautus, T. Maccius. "*Miles Gloriosus*." In *The Comedies of Plautus*, translated by Henry Thomas Riley, 69–142. London: Bell, 1912.
Pliny the Elder. *The Natural History*. Translated by. John Bostock and H. T. Riley. London: Bell, 1893.
Plutarch. "Alexander." In *Plutarch's Lives: Demosthenes and Cicero, Alexander and Caesar*, translated by Bernadotte Perrin, 7:223–440. Cambridge: Harvard University Press. 1919.
———. "The Life of Demetrius." In *Plutarch's Lives: Demetrius and Antony. Pyrrhus and Gaius Marius*, translated by Bernadotte Perrin, 9:1–136. Cambridge: Harvard University Press, 1920.
Polyaenus, *Strategems of War*. Translated by R. Shepherd. Pall-Mall: George Nicol, 1793.
Polybius. *The Histories, Volume 3*. Translated by W. P. Paton. London: William Heineman, 1972.
———. *The Histories, Volume 5*. Translated by W. P. Paton. London: William Heineman, 1972.
Rogers, Guy MacLean. *The Mysteries of Artemis of Ephesos: Cult, Polis, and Change in the Graeco-Roman World*. New Haven: Yale University Press, 2013.
Safrai, S. and M. Stern, eds. *The Jewish People in the First Century: Historical Geography, Political History, Social, Cultural and Religious Life and Institutions*. 2 vols. Compendia Rerum Iudaicarum ad Novum Testamentum 1/2. Assen: Van Gorcum, 1974.

BIBLIOGRAPHY

Scherrer, Peter. "The City of Ephesos from the Roman Period to Late Antiquity." In *Ephesos, Metropolis of Asia*, 1–26. Valley Forge: Harvard Theological Studies, 1995.

Sheedy, Kenneth. "Ephesus as Temple-Warden." https://www.mq.edu.au/research/research-centres-groups-and-facilities/resilient-societies/centres/australian-centre-for-ancient-numismatic-studies/exhibitions/the-coinage-of-ephesus/ephesus-as-temple-warden.

Sinn, Ulrich. "Greek Sanctuaries as Places of Refuge." In *Greek Sanctuaries: New Approaches*, edited by Nanno Marinatos and Robin Hagg, 142–52. London: Routledge, 1993.

Skarmintzo, Stephanos. "The Cult of Artemis in Ephesus and the Possible Explanation of the Bee Symbol." *Acta Archaeologica Pultuskiensia* 6 (2017) 269–272.

Strabo. *The Geography of Strabo*. 8 vols. Translated by Horace L Jones. Cambridge: Harvard University Press, 1917–33.

Strelan, Rick. *Paul, Artemis, and the Jews*. Berlin: de Gruyter, 1996.

Suetonius, Gius. *The Twelve Caesars*. Translated by Robert Graves. London: Folio, 1964.

Tacitus. "The Annals." In *Complete Works of Tacitus*, translated by Alfred John Church and William Jackson Brodribb, 3–416. New York: Random, 1964.

Tatius, Achilles. *The Adventures of Leucippe and Clitophon*. Translated by S. Gaselee. London: William Heineman, 1917.

Thomas, Christine. "At Home in the City of Artemis: Religion in Ephesos in the Literary Imagination of the Roman Period." In *Ephesos, Metropolis of Asia*, 81–118. Valley Forge: Harvard Theological Studies, 1995.

Thűr, Hilke. "The Processional Way in Ephesos as a Place of Cult and Burial." In *Ephesos, Metropolis of Asia*, 157–99. Valley Forge: Harvard Theological Studies, 1995.

Towner, P. H. "Gnosis and Realized Eschatology in Ephesus (of the Pastoral Epistles) and the Corinthian Enthusiasm." *Journal for the Study of the New Testament* 31 (1987) 95–124.

Trebilco, Paul. *The Early Christians in Ephesus from Paul to Ignatius*. Grand Rapids: Eerdmans, 2007.

———. *Jewish Communities in Asia Minor*. Cambridge: Cambridge University Press, 1991.

Trombley, Frank R. "Paganism in the Greek World at the End of Antiquity: The Case for Rural Anatolia and Greece." *Harvard Theological Review* 78 (1985) 327–52.

Van der Linde, Dies. "Artemis Ephesia, The Emperor and the City: Impact of the Imperial Cult and the Civic Identity of Roman Ephesos." *Ancient Society* 46 (2016) 165–201.

Varro. *On the Latin Language, Volume 2*. Translated by Roland G. Trent. Cambridge: Harvard University Press, 1938.

Vitruvius, Marcus Pollio. *On Architecture*. Translated by Morris Hickey Morgan. Dover: New York, 1960.

BIBLIOGRAPHY

Walters, James C. "Egyptian Religions in Ephesos." In *Ephesos, Metropolis of Asia*, 281-309. Valley Forge: Harvard Theological Studies, 1995.

White, L. Michael. "Urban Development and Social Change in Ephesos." In *Ephesos, Metropolis of Asia*, 281-309. Valley Forge: Harvard Theological Studies, 1995.

Xenophon of Ephesus. "An Ephesian Tale." In *Anthology of Ancient Greek Popular Literature*, translated by Moses Hadas, 3-49. Bloomington: Indiana University Press, 1998.

Yamauchi, Edwin M. *Pre-Christian Gnosticism*. 2nd ed. Grand Rapids: Barker, 1983.

Zabehlicky, Heinrich. "Preliminary Views of the Ephesian Harbour." In *Ephesos, Metropolis of Asia*, 201-16. Valley Forge: Harvard Theological Studies, 1995.

www.ingramcontent.com/pod-product-compliance
Lightning Source LLC
Chambersburg PA
CBHW050835160426
43192CB00010B/2040